DATE DUE

DEMCO 38-296

REACHING A
MULTICULTURAL
STUDENT COMMUNITY

Reaching a Multicultural Student Community

A HANDBOOK FOR ACADEMIC LIBRARIANS

Karen E. Downing,
Barbara MacAdam,
and
Darlene P. Nichols

The Greenwood Library Management Collection

GREENWOOD PRESS
Westport, Connecticut • London

Library of Congress Cataloging-in-Publication Data

Downing, Karen E.
    Reaching a multicultural student community : a handbook for
academic librarians / Karen E. Downing, Barbara MacAdam, and Darlene
P. Nichols.
        p.   cm.—(The Greenwood library management collection, ISSN
0894–2986)
    Includes bibliographical references and index.
    ISBN 0–313–27912–8 (alk. paper)
    1. Library orientation for minority college students—United
States.   2. Peer counseling of students—United States.
    I. MacAdam, Barbara.   II. Nichols, Darlene P.   III. Title.
    IV. Series.
    Z711.2.D68   1993
    025.5'67708'693—dc20   93–548

British Library Cataloguing in Publication Data is available.

Library of Congress Catalog Card Number: 93–548
ISBN: 0–313–27912–8
ISSN: 0894–2986

First published in 1993

Greenwood Press, 88 Post Road West, Westport, CT 06881
An imprint of Greenwood Publishing Group, Inc.

Printed in the United States of America

The paper used in this book complies with the
Permanent Paper Standard issued by the National
Information Standards Organization (Z39.48–1984).

10 9 8 7 6 5 4 3 2 1

Contents

Illustrations

FIGURES

TABLES

Preface

In 1985, the University of Michigan Undergraduate Library (UGL) received funding from the university's Office of Academic Affairs to begin an experimental library-based program targeted to the needs of minority students. The program was to be a mechanism for students to learn skills in information handling and microcomputer use from other students. Three assumptions supported the program's design: (1) that library research and information-handling skills, like writing and analytical thinking, are part of the foundation for a successful academic experience; (2) that a large research library, which is often an intimidating and confusing world to the student population at large, may be especially troublesome to minority students; and (3) that one of the best resources for helping minority students succeed is the influence of successful minority students themselves.

The University of Michigan's Peer Information Counseling program (PIC) employs minority undergraduate students to teach information-handling and microcomputer skills, and to serve as role models for minority students who might initially feel more comfortable asking for assistance from another minority student than from a librarian. Specific objectives for the program include:

- furthering the use of the library and of microcomputers by minority students;
- improving the information-handling skills and computer skills of minority students;

- developing the information-handling, computer, and counseling skills of the students hired as counselors; and

- contributing to a campus atmosphere that promotes retention of minority undergraduates.

The Office of the Vice President for Academic Affairs provided funding for the first three years of the project, subsequently making the funding part of the library's base budget. Support included an assistant librarian's salary, $10,000 per year in PIC student salaries, $2,000 for supplies, and the initial outlay for two microcomputers: an IBM-compatible Zenith and a Macintosh. PIC program personnel initially consisted of five minority undergraduates supervised by a minority librarian as program coordinator. During the 1985–86 academic year, seven minority students worked as Peer Information Counselors. All were highly motivated juniors or seniors active in the university minority communities and interested in the success of the program. They included economics, biology, and English majors, and most had plans to go on to graduate or professional school.

Activities of the PIC students fell into five general areas:

- assisting patrons at the reference desk,

- tutoring students in word processing,

- providing in-depth term paper assistance,

- producing instructional materials, and

- publicizing the PIC program.

The greatest challenge facing the program was gaining the visibility and recognition among faculty and students necessary to maximize use of the services by targeted groups. Some of Michigan's characteristics as an institution created impediments to program growth: Its size, pluralism, diversity, and tradition of decentralization and autonomy among its component schools and departments all conspired to make it difficult to implement a direct and immediate line of contact among students, faculty members, and instructional support programs. Minority student support programs also reflect this diversity and decentralization. There was no niche into which PIC could easily fit.

The interest, questions, and suggestions from librarians over the last five years about the Peer Information Counseling program (see Appendix One) suggested the need for a practical book on the design and implementation of such a program. This handbook is intended for academic librarians who are interested in establishing peer outreach programs for minority students on their campuses, or are trying to decide whether such a program would meet the needs of their students. Chapters include an overview of the unique challenges facing academic institutions and libraries today in serving the "new majority," suggestions on working effectively in the current academic environment, and practical guidelines for specific program design, implementation, and evaluation. We hope this book will be useful for both experienced program planners and administrators, as well as for the librarian new to the ins and outs of program development.

REACHING A
MULTICULTURAL
STUDENT COMMUNITY

1

Introduction

On college campuses throughout the country, students, faculty, and administrators are engaged, both by choice and by external pressure, in a reexamination of what it means to have a college education. The portraits of a "typical" college student, what constitutes a "core" liberal arts curriculum, what constitutes fair and equal access to educational opportunity, what constitute legitimate areas of scholarship, even what deserves to come under the label "great book," are changing. Change is never easy, and campuses have been rocked by debate, often hostile and painful. No one disagrees that the old sureties and givens of the past are eroding, but it is much easier to recognize an outdated vision than to shape a new and distinct one. "Multiculturalism," "diversity," "pluralism," "nontraditional," "students at risk," "gender studies," "canon"—the list could go on indefinitely, but the rhetoric evolving to describe the changing environment in educational institutions defines one, clear-cut commonality. There is no longer a typical college student, nor the illusion that the aggregate assumptions that formerly provided a comfortable stereotype of such a student will ever obtain in quite the same way. White, middle to upper class 18 to 22 years old, supported by parental money or readily obtainable student loans, living in dormitories or on-campus housing, and selecting predictable majors along gender lines—these descriptors no longer constitute a valid demographic picture of the potential incoming college student, and that picture may all but disappear over the next several decades (Commission on Minority Participation; Kravitz, Rios, and Sykes). Instead, the entering college student is likely to enroll later in life, to return to school after time spent in the workplace, to be Native American, black, Hispanic, Asian, multiracial, female, or nonhetero-sexual, to speak English as a second language, to bring a non–Western European cultural perspective, or to be at risk for academic failure due to a complex set of economic, social, academic, and cultural barriers inherent in institutions of higher education. This range of cultural, ethnic, and racial identity that will characterize future student popula-tions defines the "diverse" or "multicultural" student community.

Academic librarians, no less than other administrators, faculty, and policy makers on college campuses, are faced with the challenge of planning and providing services and programs for undergraduate students in a multicultural environment. They are also offered the unique challenge of providing leadership within the campus community and the community of higher education in changing and redefining the institutional environ-ment. To do so effectively, librarians must also be willing to alter long-held assumptions about their primary clientele or the average student user and be willing to explore equally innovative responses to the needs of a multicultural student community. Libraries that fail to consider the needs of the new undergraduates run the risk of becoming increasingly marginal and inaccessible to students (Stoffle). Smaller institutions, particularly liberal arts colleges devoted to undergraduate teaching, have long served as successful models in supporting and educating students as individuals. For librarians in larger institutions, particularly public or urban univer-sities, to reach the student body as a whole will mean following the models of outreach increasingly established by institutions themselves. This means developing programs specifically designed to reach students as individuals and to help break down the institutional barriers that make students feel alienated and militate against their academic success. This volume provides an institutional context for the multicultural campus community as well as practical help for academic librarians in planning, implementing, and evaluating special outreach programs designed for culturally, ethnically, and racially diverse students.

CAMPUSES IN A MULTICULTURAL SOCIETY

At the heart of the changes currently taking place on campuses is an underlying tension between the efforts of institutions to recruit a multicul-tural student body representative of the population as a whole, and the ability of these institutions to retain and graduate these students. Richardson and Skinner (1991) describe this underlying tension as intra-institutional conflict over achieving cultural diversity at the perceived expense of "quality." (Motivated by good intentions, yet ambivalent regarding the consequences of institutional transformation, academic institutions often regard wider admissions policies and the students thus admitted with suspicion.) Students are recruited on the basis of past educational achievement and perhaps precisely because of their cultural affiliations, but then are expected to succeed in an environment in which they are made to feel marginalized, alienated, and academically unprepared. Presenting case studies of academic institutions successful not only in enrolling minority students but in creating an environment of academic success, Richardson and Skinner describe a model of institutional adaptation to student diversity. In this model universities go through three stages—reactive, strategic, and adaptive—the final stage representing critical change in the institutional climate (in curriculum content and pedagogy, for example), thus eradicating many of the factors that present insurmountable barriers to graduation. Libraries play a large role in creating this institutional climate and have a key role to play in fashioning change. Academic librarians must understand that they will go through the same organizational conflicts over philosophy, methodology, institutional mission, and resource allocation as does the parent institution. Further, to work effectively within the institutional framework as both participants and leaders, librarians must have a clear sense of which of these three stages currently characterizes their institution. Finally, to work effectively on the multicultural campus, librarians must also identify, assess, and adapt strategies and program models from other academic support sectors.

INFORMATION LITERACY AND THE MULTICULTURAL CAMPUS

In response to *A Nation at Risk* (U.S. National Commission) and other reports on national education reform that ignored the role of libraries in an information society, a 1989 report from the American Library Association Presidental Committee on Information Literacy defined information-literate persons as "those who are able to recognize when information is needed and have the ability to locate, evaluate, and use effectively the needed information" (American Library Association Presidential Committee on Information Literacy, 1989, 1). In her literature review on information literacy in the academic library context, Trish Ridgeway (1990) cites numerous articles that underscore the vital importance of information skills as part of the foundation of the academic experience as well as their importance for lifelong learning and adaptation in our information-dependent society. Understanding the elements critical to information literacy and recognizing the peculiar barriers presented by modern academic libraries to the multicultural student are essential precursors to library program planning.

The information literate student should be able to:
- define information needs;
- analyze, identify, and retrieve information effectively;
- critically evaluate information for bias, relevance, and importance;
- synthesize, organize, and present information orally and in writing;
- work effectively within electronic information systems.

Barriers to information literacy for multicultural students include:
- language
- technology
- limited prior access to libraries
- pedagogy designed for the cognitive styles of "typical" students
- information systems established around unfamiliar conceptual frameworks.

Harder to delineate are effective strategies for fostering information literacy among students, particularly multicultural students. Students who arrive on campus having had limited library experience and few opportunities to use microcomputers or other technology are less likely to view traditional library collections as accessible or meaningful, and are apt to be marginal or unwilling library users. The first goal may be to bring the library and the student together in a productive relationship. Across the country, academic libraries have developed multicultural or diversity librarian positions as a significant first step in reaching out actively to the multicultural user community (Dyson).

OUTREACH: A BROADER VISION OF USER INSTRUCTION

A review of *C&RL News* from 1988 through 1991 chronicles numerous workshops, programs, and symposia related to multiculturalism and academic libraries. The issues range broadly from building multicultural collections to recruiting and retaining a multicultural staff. Increasingly, however, attention has been directed to the specific challenge of designing user instruction targeted to the needs of the multicultural student (Mensching; American Library Association ACRL/BIS). Such questions include how culture affects learning styles, alternative conceptual frameworks, and the increased emphasis on the role of critical inquiry in evolving curriculum related to racial, ethnic, or gender studies. Adding to the current reexamination of bibliographic instruction is another emerging theme: outreach (Downing and Nagaraja). Long the presumed territory of public libraries, outreach in academic libraries is predicated on the assumption that the changing library environment and changing library users provide new opportunities and new obligations to bring information, services, and help to students. Remote electronic access to expanding information utilities, from the online catalog to national bulletin boards, is an ever more likely possibility for students in academic libraries. Paradoxically, however, the proliferation of electronic information, often devoid of the more familiar signposts and filters found in traditional print sources, has created another barrier for students, especially those disadvantaged by lack of exposure to technology and intimidated by the unfamiliar landscape of academia. If remote system access offers virtually unlimited information resources to the multicultural student, outreach programs are a bridge between students and the library, assuring them the personal and academic support critical to their effective use of information. Students less familiar with the range of resources available in the library, less confident in their ability to use technology, and more likely to feel daunted and alienated by the academic research library cannot be expected to initiate productive encounters with the library. Outreach programs draw upon a repertory of effective strategies to establish, maintain, and enrich contacts with students beyond the reference desk and the classroom.

USING STUDENTS TO REACH STUDENTS

Peer counseling or peer assistance as a concept has come to play a key role in many social support programs, increasingly so in colleges and universities (Russel and Skinkle, 388). Peer help is predicated on the assumption that in many circumstances one can be greatly helped by an individual not so very different from oneself, someone who has been through similar experiences and understands not only the difficulties involved, but also how the other person might feel and react. Perceived differences in status between two people can create barriers to effective communication, particularly in situations where one of the individuals feels vulnerable, threatened, or powerless. On college campuses, students frequently serve as volunteers in services ranging from peer-tutoring programs for math and science to crisis counseling hot-lines. Students from a cultural background different from that of the majority population are less likely than other students to encounter faculty, staff, and students who share their culture, value system, concerns, and interests. Minority students in particular may find that they rely more on each other and on personal networks of family, minority faculty, and minority advisors than do majority students. Tinto describes the dilemma minority students encounter: "Beyond the existence of possible discrimination, minority students generally, and black students in particular, may find it especially difficult to find and become a member of a supportive community within a college" (1987, 71). Except in institutions where recruiting and retaining minority faculty and staff have been made a high priority, students will have few interactions in the library with staff who understand their needs or can easily bridge the perceived distance between the student and the academic enclave.

Experience suggests that the use of minority students as peer counselors, by fostering a greater sense of membership in the university community, can overcome several of the barriers to effective library use by multicultural students (Russel and Skinkle, 392). As shapers of and participants in outreach programs, students can build upon established networks so essential to the fabric of the multicultural community. In their role as library staff, minority students provide the diverse role models and support structure so often lacking in academic institutions. As partners in academic support efforts within the library, minority students can help library staff better understand the feelings and needs of the multicultural student community.

ISSUES FOR LIBRARIANS

As academic librarians begin the process of self-scrutiny and user redefinition necessary to effective program building for multicultural students, it is important to understand the factors that will contribute to success and the challenges that must be overcome. Program innovation of any kind in today's beleaguered academic library comes at the expense of other activities. Faced with staff cuts, serials budgets in crisis, increased reliance even in publicly supported institutions on external fund-raising, and the ongoing demands of emerging technologies, librarians are hard-pressed to maintain daily operations and continue well-established services and programs. The tendency in such an organizational environment is to hang on tightly to the status quo, attempting, with the best of intentions, to identify "core" or "basic" activities at the expense of innovation. The changing portrait of America's campuses, however, argues powerfully for change and program innovation. Librarians must be prepared to make difficult decisions on resource allocation and cannot assume that additional program money will be forthcoming, either within the library or institution or from external sources. They must further expect to deal with hard questions from skeptical colleagues and administrators concerned with budgets, overextended staff, and institutional priorities. Librarians might also find themselves expected to devise programs or services for multicultural students under the pressures of an institutional mission or redirection, but without the practical support necessary for successful program building and assessment.

The debate surrounding multiculturalism in education is no less intense than concerns over resource allocation on college campuses. Librarians might find themselves upbraided for pandering to the tyranny of "political correctness" at the same time they are castigated for failing to respond quickly enough to the needs of the multicultural community. Many faculty and students may be ambivalent about the changes they perceive the library is making in old and familiar ways and worry that "special" programs may divert attention and resources from collections or services they value.

It is crucial to be clear about the overall goals of such program development and to frame goals in the context of institutional commitment. As with any new endeavor, staff must expect initial failures, small and large, and be ready to make adaptations and set new directions when necessary. Staff must also be prepared for the responsibilities of success as new relationships with users develop. The end result of hard work and commitment is a library that truly serves the range of needs presented by diverse users.

ESTABLISHING A MINORITY OUTREACH PROGRAM

Academic librarians in each institution must decide on the needs of their student user community and the most effective ways to meet those needs. A peer-based outreach program tailored to campus needs is one such solution. Figures 1.1 and 1.2 and Tables 1.1 and 1.2 outline possible program components, and succeeding chapters offer practical suggestions for the design and implementation of such a program.

Figure 1.1
Roles of Peer Information Counselors

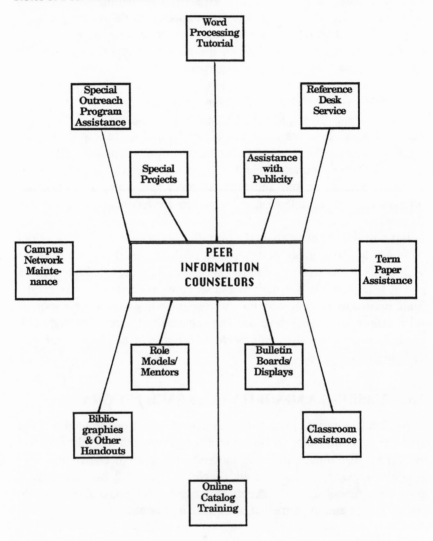

Table 1.1
Description of Peer Counselor Tasks

Word Processing Tutorials: Either regularly scheduled drop-in hours or by appointment, this service is likely to be the only place on campus where a student (who may be computer phobic, or did not have the opportunity to use computers in high school) can get one-on-one training by a peer in how to use software.

Publicity Assistance: Peer counselors can assist in your publicity efforts in many ways: They can post flyers, hand out give-aways, assist with mass mailings, etc.

Reference Desk Service: Peer counselors are perhaps most helpful at a busy visible public service point such as a reference desk. Here they help other students find the resources they need and serve as role models to other students.

Term Paper Assistance: More experienced peer counselors may wish to assist with students in more depth than is usually allowed at the reference desk. They may wish to assist with one-on-one term paper counseling by appointment.

Classroom Assistance: Peer counselors can totally change the classroom environment by making others feel more comfortable asking questions, and encouraged to see a peer who has a firm grasp of the concepts and tools being taught.

Bulletin Boards: Who better to know what will be interesting to undergraduates than other students? Peer counselors can put together fun and informative displays on any topic.

Online Catalog Training: Computerized catalogs can be very intimidating to undergraduate students. One-on-one tutorials on how to use the online catalog or CD-ROM products give students the confidence and basic or advanced knowledge they need to access materials they need.

Role Models/Mentors: Whether at the reference desk, in the classroom, or doing outreach, peer counselors will serve as role models to the students they serve. It is important they realize other students will look to them for assistance and encouragement.

Handouts and Bibliography Composition: Peer counselors can assist full-time staff in putting together point of use handouts, pathfinders, and bibliographies on any topic. It is a nice service to offer pathfinders or bibliographies on people of color since locating material on these groups is often difficult and time-consuming.

Campus Network Building & Maintenance: Peer counselors can assist with the network building that is so vital to a healthy library program. They can visit departments and units with full-time staff, deliver program brochures around campus, and represent the library at campus events.

Special Outreach Programs: Peer counselors should be included in all library outreach efforts. Whether it is a program in a residence hall, an open house, or an orientation session, peer counselors add wonderful insights to the program.

Special Projects: With their knowledge and insight into how students function and the workings of the library, peer counselors are great sources to tap into when special projects arise. Projects such as surveying users for program evaluation, information gathering for special reports, etc., all could benefit from the input of peer counselors.

Figure 1.2
Roles of Program Coordinator

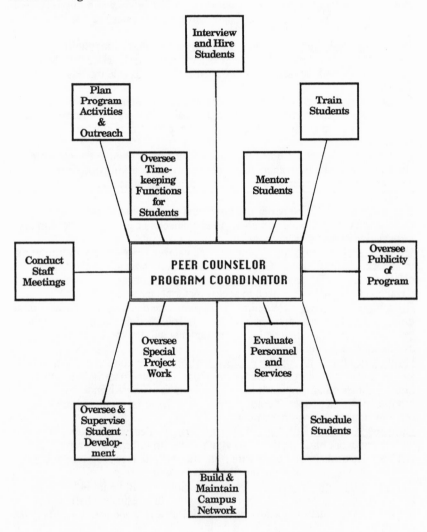

Interview and Hire Students

Plan Program Activities & Outreach

Train Students

Oversee Time-keeping Functions for Students

Mentor Students

Conduct Staff Meetings

PEER COUNSELOR PROGRAM COORDINATOR

Oversee Publicity of Program

Oversee Special Project Work

Evaluate Personnel and Services

Oversee & Supervise Student Development

Schedule Students

Build & Maintain Campus Network

Table 1.2
Description of Coordinators' Tasks

Interview and Hire Students: This must be done at the beginning of each academic year. Try to get a one-year commitment from students so that it need only be done just once per year.

Mentor Students: Must create an approachable and caring environment in which peer counselors of all backgrounds will feel comfortable accepting assistance and advice from coordinator. Take an active and sincere interest in their lives and goals.

Train Students: Comprehensive training sessions must be planned and documented. Supplemental training sessions should occur throughout the year.

Evaluate Personnel & Services: Evaluation of peers should be as positive and nonintimidating as possible. Both formal and informal methods should be used. Evaluation of services should occur on a periodic basis. The coordinator may wish to recruit peers to help with evaluation.

Oversee Publicity of Program: Every type of publicity that is affordable and appropriate should be considered. Again, enlisting the help of peers to determine the best mix of publicity will be beneficial.

Schedule Students: Initial schedule should be set at beginning of each semester. Cover most important hours first, then fill in secondary hours as available. Ask students to find their own substitutes to protect coordinator's time.

Build & Maintain Campus Network: A constant challenge and an enjoyable part of coordinating a program; regular contact with lay people around campus will go a long way towards promoting your services.

Oversee & Supervise Student Development: Develop on ongoing training and development plan for peers. Once they have a kit of experience, allow them to do more of a variety of duties.

Oversee Special Project Work: If money allows, have select students work independently on special projects such as creating flyers, bibliographies, and pathfinders.

Conduct Staff Meetings: At regular intervals throughout the academic year, the coordinator will want to hold meetings where all the peers can attend. At the initial organizational meeting at the beginning of the year, determine when peers can all meet.

Timekeeping: Coordinator must keep meticulous records of weekly payroll in case there are problems. Ask a trusted peer to assist with this process if financially feasible.

Plan Program Activities & Outreach: Regular outreach activities should be planned throughout the year as a service to students, and to help publicize the program. Enlist assistance of peers for programming ideas and implementation. Tie activities into other programs on campus.

REFERENCES

American Library Association, Association of College and Research Libraries, Bibliographic Instruction Section. "Cultural Diversity and Higher Education: BI in a Multicultural Environment." Preconference held at the annual meeting of the American Library Association, Atlanta, June 28, 1991.

American Library Association Presidential Committee on Information Literacy. *Final Report*. Chicago: American Library Association, January 1989.

Commission on Minority Participation in Education and American Life. *One Third of a Nation*. Washington, D.C.: ACE/Education Commission of the States, 1988.

Downing, Karen, and Jayashri Nagaraja. "Innovation and Outreach in Academic Libraries." Forthcoming.

Dyson, Alan. "Reraching Out for Outreach: A University Library Develops a New Position to Serve the School's Multicultural Students." *American Libraries*, November 1989, 952–54.

Kravitz, Lesley, Adela Terres Rios, and Vivian B. Sykes. "Documenting Their Voices: Building Library Collections for the New Majority." *Journal of Library Administration and Management*, November 1991.

MacAdam, Barbara, and Darlene Nichols. "Peer Information Counseling: An Academic Library Program for Minority Students." *Journal of Academic Librarianship* 15 (September 1989), 204–9.

————. "Peer Information Counseling at the University of Michigan Undergraduate Library." *Journal of Academic Librarianship*, May 1988, 80–81.

Mensching, Theresa B., ed. *Reaching and Teaching Diverse Library User Groups*. Ann Arbor, Mich.: Pierian Press, 1989.

Richardson, Richard C., and Elizabeth Fisk Skinner. *Achieving Quality and Diversity: Universities in a Multicultural Society*. New York: American Council on Education, 1991.

Ridgeway, Trish. "Information Literacy: An Introductory Reading List." *C&RL News*, July/August 1990, 645–48.

Russel, John H., and Rodney R. Skinkle. "Evaluation of Peer Advisor Effectiveness." *Journal of College Student Development*, September 1990, 388–93.

Stoffle, Carla J. "A New Library for the New Undergraduate." *Library Journal* 115, no. 16 (October 1, 1990), 47–51.

Tinto, Vincent. *Leaving College: Rethinking the Causes and Cures of Student Attrition*. Chicago: University of Chicago Press, 1987.

U.S. National Commission on Excellence in Education. *A Nation at Risk*. Washington, D.C.: Government Printing Office, 1983.

2

Community Analysis

The population of the United States is changing rapidly. In the 1960s and 70s, the baby boomers began to come of age and produce offspring of their own. But this generation was different from that of its parents. Birthrates were lower, and the typical 1950s families of three, four, or more children were replaced by smaller families with one or two children. Overall, the birthrate has declined in the United States. For some subgroups of the population, however, this has not held true. Minority birthrates have continued to increase in the post–baby boom period, and immigrants—legal and illegal—from countries such as Mexico and Vietnam continue to arrive in large numbers. Entering college classes will likely have a new look in the next decade.

Projections from the 1980 census suggested that the total number of 18-year-olds (the modal age for college entrance) would decline between 1979 and 1998 from over four and a half million to about three and a half million (Solmon and Wingard, 23). In fact, in the 1990 census, the number of 18-year-olds had already dropped to just over three and a half million. As this total has dropped, the percentage of nonwhite 18-year-olds has increased from approximately 20 percent to almost 25 percent and is likely to go even higher. In the 1990s, therefore, colleges may see greater numbers of nonwhite applicants and enrollees.

Unfortunately, however, the consequences of these changing demographics are not in fact so straightforward or clear-cut. While high school completion rates for black and Hispanic students rose between 1974 and 1985, the percentage progressing into college after graduation actually

Table 2.1
Educational Attainment Rate Comparison

	Year	High School Completion	Progression into College
Black	1974	55.8%	41.6%
	1985	62.8%	38.5%
Hispanic	1974	48.9%	49.0%
	1985	49.9%	44.7%
White	1974	76.2%	45.0%
	1985	76.7%	55.9%

declined at the same time (Solmon and Wingard, 25–26). These rates have been summarized in Table 2.1.

High minority teen birthrates, financial pressures, poor academic preparation, lack of family or other role models, and many other social circumstances contribute to low college progression and low graduation rates among minority youth. Though interest in these problems has increased, and piecemeal efforts to address them have been made, little change is likely in the 1990s without massive across-the-board social and educational reform. Colleges and universities will need to make changes in their recruitment efforts, in their assumptions about new students, and in the support programs provided for these students. There are other implications for higher education in the upcoming decade as well: more money will be needed for remediation of inadequately prepared students, and more resources will have to be devoted to counseling and advising them (Solmon and Wingard, 29).

Once these students are in college, there is the challenge of retaining them through graduation. A national study undertaken in 1987 by the National Institute of Independent Colleges and Universities determined that the dropout rate six years after enrollment for all students was 44.5 percent. For black students the rate was 63.3 percent, and for Hispanic students 54.4 percent (Porter, 13). Many reasons are cited for this dropout rate: lack of money and the need to begin working are probably most prominent. Other reasons include discomfort with the institutional environment and academic failure. The institution can address all of these problems to some degree, and each unit within the institution can contribute to improving the experiences of at-risk minority students and increasing their chances of reaching graduation.

College and university libraries affect students at all levels and across all academic disciplines. Sooner or later, most students pass through the library's doors. The library is in a singular position to have an impact on a large segment of the campus population. It is interesting that, in a literature search on the impact of changing demographics on academic libraries, very little comes up. Libraries are often viewed as reactive institutions, waiting for external pressures before beginning internal changes. Forward-looking changes are often difficult to promote and slow to be implemented in large, bureaucratic academic institutions. Here, however, is an opportunity for librarians to take a proactive stance and to help set the pace, not only for other libraries, but also for the larger institution they serve.

The implications of demographic change are wide-ranging. There are implications for the collection in terms of the subject coverage and reading level. If the college or university is providing remedial or "booster" programs, the library needs to support such programs with appropriate and accessible materials. There are implications for library instruction programs and similar services: for example, the library might want to provide its own remediation programs and link them to similar programs on campus. Probably most students who enter college have only a rudimentary idea of how to use a college or university library—their skills generally stop at author/title/subject searching in the catalog and *Readers' Guide to Periodical Literature*; some students have not had the benefit of even that much instruction or access to resources such as *Readers' Guide*. As libraries become more and more high tech, librarians are also likely to see students with weak high school academic backgrounds falling further and further behind their peers from other institutions. There are additional implications for staffing: students may feel more comfortable working with another minority person or may need someone with special language skills such as Spanish or Hmong. The potential impact on collections, service, and personnel is tremendous. Demographically, the U.S. population is changing rapidly and will continue to change. Librarians need to begin preparing for the changes today.

COMMUNITY ANALYSIS—DEFINING THE COMMUNITY

Community analysis is a management planning tool that "embraces the study of two elements: community characteristics, and the significance of these characteristics" (Evans, 441). Unless a librarian is new to the library, he or she is likely to have an idea of what the community is like. But doing a community analysis will lead to a truer and fuller understanding: "one main purpose of community analysis is to substitute facts for guesses" (Goldhor, 302). It also substitutes facts for the assumptions and misconceptions that planners may have.

The community analysis will have at least two final products: a picture of what the community looks like and a list of the community's needs. It is like putting together a puzzle to reveal a complete picture. Many pieces go into the final assembly, and the loss of one piece will make the picture incomplete. The more information available, the better one can understand the community and make solid and meaningful decisions. Many formal and informal mechanisms exist for accomplishing this task.

At the outset planners should define the target community, that is, what group is to be analyzed? This may not be as straightforward as it at first appears. Any institution will have several layers of "community" that need to be understood to arrive at a complete picture. Start with the core group of any institution of higher education, the students, and work outward to include other constituent groups in order to better see the whole. This makes it easier to see where the library fits in and where it can have an impact on the community.

The Students

Efforts to assemble a community analysis will naturally focus on the student body. Although the library may intend to concentrate programming on a particular subset of the student population, initially the community analysis should include information about the entire student body. The subset can then be placed in a broader context. Insofar as possible the analysis should help to identify how the subset group differs from the student body at large in order to help determine what needs the group may have. Keep in mind, though, that as much as they may differ, there will be many similarities. It is also important to continuously remind oneself that the numbers describe the aggregate, but may not have anything to do with specific individuals encountered by the library staff. Not all members of the target group will need special programming. And certainly there will be students outside of the group who could benefit greatly from any of the library's special services.

Educational institutions tend to collect many descriptive statistics; it should be possible, therefore, to draw together a detailed picture of the campus population from the statistics gathered by offices across campus. The admissions office may be able to provide information on applicants and on those who are admitted. The registrar keeps data on those who are currently enrolled. Some campuses have other offices as well: minority services or affirmative action offices, for example. The president's office and the campus publications department are other sources for information. In large institutions information is likely to be distributed over several offices or service points. A look through the campus directory will help to identify possible sources of information. (See Table 2.2 for a summary of potential sources and the information they may be able to provide.) Each source may also be able to offer references to other sources. This search for information may also be the seed of a campus network of contacts to promote, evaluate, and develop the new program.

Table 2.2
Some Sources of Information for the Community Analysis

Library   The library may hold and archive campus publications such as the following:
                              college catalogs
                              student publications (newspapers, etc.)
                              administrative documents (Five-Year Plan, etc.)
                              publications directed to alumni

                              The library may also have local, state, or regional census data, and state and local documents.

Admissions
Office   Can provide at least numbers on how many students have applied and have been admitted. Will probably keep data on demographic breakdown as well (e.g., number of minority students who have applied, breakdown by state of residence, etc.)

Registrar's
Office   Usually keeps detailed information about students who are currently enrolled. Will probably have a detailed breakdown by state of residence, minority status, sex, school or department, part-time/full-time status, etc. Some of this information may be considered confidential or require a special procedure to request.

Other Administrative
Offices   These might include offices devoted to student affairs, academic affairs, minority affairs, Affirmative Action, services to international students, to students with disabilities, to gay and lesbian students, etc. Offices of the president, vice-presidents, and deans are additional sources of information on faculty, students, and special services. They may be able to provide documents on institutional goals and objectives, plans, and current state of affairs.

Academic
Departments   Information about faculty: numbers, ranks, teaching load, tenure; information about numbers of students enrolled in classes, and number of majors; information about required courses or most popular courses.

If data are hard to retrieve, informal sources may be able to help: many campuses have minority student organizations such as those for black or Hispanic students. These organizations may not be able to provide exact numbers, but they probably will have a good approximate idea. Student advisors and others who have close contact with students can often provide some answers as well. Informal communication with staff in admissions and elsewhere may be fruitful if the institution is hesitant to distribute statistics.

In addition to straight population figures, a number of other characteristics are useful to consider:

- Where do the students live? On or off campus? Do they have long commutes or live nearby?
- Where are they from? Rural communities, suburbs, inner cities?
- What are their majors? Largely humanities, social sciences, sciences?
- What is their financial aid picture? Are many of them working? If so, how many hours?
- What kind of high schools did they attend?
- What percentage is part-time?

Of course, the registrar or admissions staff will not have the answers to all these questions. Counselors, academic advisors, and faculty members, however, will have impressions worth including in the final picture. Officers or members of student organizations can provide other pieces of the puzzle. Residence hall or dormitory staff members, student publications and their staffs, and student government members represent other resources as well.

The Faculty

Ideally, the faculty will play an important role in promoting library services by referring students to them. It is useful, therefore, to have a sense of faculty composition, distribution, and patterns of library use on behalf of students (e.g., bibliographic instruction or course reserves).

The president's office or the unit in charge of academic affairs may be able to provide information about faculty makeup. Some departments might also be willing to share general information with the library. This information might well include numbers of faculty at different levels as well as the number of graduate students employed to teach undergraduates.

Faculty data can hint at a number of areas of concern. For example, if you have data on the size and distribution of the faculty compared to the distribution of undergraduate majors, it is possible to get a sense of how much individual attention and assistance a student might get. Or faculty members who do not use many library services may not quickly catch on to new library initiatives, and the library may need to develop special marketing techniques. Such indicators can help add another piece to the puzzle.

The Institutional and Academic Environment

The library program will support the students' academic activities. Program planners should have a sense of the range of courses available (this may be extensive), key courses in various departments, courses required of all students, special programs, and where the strengths of the academic institution lie.

Identify the special services that are already present within the university or college structure by going through directories, the college catalog, or other publications, and by asking students and faculty members. Asking for data from staff members involved with student services provides the opportunity to ask other questions as well. Find out what kind of support— financial or otherwise—they feel they get from the administration. Ask how they perceive the academic environment for minority students. These service providers will probably have strong opinions on what is going right on campus in efforts to improve the academic environment as well as efforts to promote diversity, what is going wrong, and what the administration should do to institute improvements.

Another facet of the academic environment is the assessment of the institutional climate. Level of campus activism and direction of campus politics may have a profound impact on any programming the library plans. On one hand, a highly politicized campus might be very welcoming of new initiatives to assist minority or other special interest groups. On the other hand, in the same environment, such new programs might be interpreted as insulting to the abilities of the target constituency. The shape of your program will be influenced in some measure by concerns and activities on campus.

Several approaches can be used to assess the institutional climate. Most employees will have a good sense of what is occurring on campus and can gain further insights by keeping up with campus media (newspapers, radio broadcasts, other publications). Talking with students—patrons or student staff members—can add another perspective. Talk to student leaders or attend rallies and other activities. Staff members in other service offices will offer important perspectives as well. Ask them, through informal conversation or formal interviews or surveys how they think new programming might be received on campus. Get out of the library to see what is happening on campus and to show interest in campus activities. Going to student dorms and the offices of faculty and staff members shows genuine interest in their views.

It will also be useful to identify the various means of communication used on campus. List the student publications and their circulation and target audiences. The institution or various departments might also have separate publications such as newsletters. Check to see how extensively electronic mail or conferencing is used. Check for bulletin boards, display cases, outdoor banners or kiosks, and other means of communicating with the target audience.

The Administration and Governing Bodies

Other bodies, too, might have some impact on the direction of campus programs. A state school may have to contend with mandates of the state legislature, for example. There may be pressure on the school to provide more support for minorities within the state. Regents or other governing bodies may be more or less supportive of such programs. Knowledge of levels of interest and support on the part of high-level governance or individuals (such as a specific regent) may help to justify new program initiatives.

The administration may also have publications that can give insights into its goals (or lack of goals) for multiculturalism on campus. Campus governance groups will probably have numerous publications outlining future plans as well as statements assessing "the state of the campus." Annual reports, texts of addresses, and texts of regental or other deliberations may have some reference to where campus governors see the institution heading regarding multiculturalism.

In addition, a program planner should assess the climate of the library itself. Determine if there are goals regarding multiculturalism or other relevant service goals. Existing programs within the library might also be used as a base for developing something new.

The Wider Community

Is the target community the population currently on campus, or do you need to think about a larger community? A state school, for example, may take as its community—the population which it serves—all of the citizens of that state. Even a private school might see itself as having regional responsibilities. A community college may limit its community to the people of its city or county. In particular, if an institution is actively looking to change its demographics, expects change in the near future, or has been mandated to provide service to a designated constituency, a community analysis will necessarily include some information about the wider community as well.

Realistically, there may not be time or staff to do an exhaustive analysis of the constituent population and institutional environment. Librarians should at least make themselves aware of the minority population statistics in their region and how they compare to those of the institution. The analysis may also include information about immigration into the state and high school graduation rates of selected groups. Regional offices, such as boards of education, should be able to provide some of this information. Census data and other government publications also offer good sources of basic information.

Some information included in the community analysis will be quantifiable; some will not. Qualitative data—including impressions, attitudes, and opinions—are just as valuable as quantitative information. Qualitative information gives the library insights into what the community is thinking. And this is part of better understanding the whole picture.

COMMUNITY ANALYSIS—COMMUNITY NEEDS

From the community analysis the library staff member will begin to develop an idea of community needs as well as a sense of what might work in the given environment. A campus where most students commute, for example, will have some library needs which differ from the needs of those campuses where most students live in dorms close to the library. Pockets of special needs may become evident as well: a contingent of students who are recent immigrants, for example, or a special academic program aimed at students with weak high school backgrounds may have been "discovered" during the community analysis. This largely numerical picture, however, cannot fully show how the campus "thinks" about multiculturalism or about the library.

In addition to facts and figures, the community analysis should include some consideration of opinions and attitudes of community members, both library users and nonusers. One way to gather that kind of information is through a survey. Though conducting a survey is labor-intensive and time-consuming, there may be a way around all the work. Some colleges and universities survey all new students at some point during the year. The administering office may be willing to include some library-related questions in an official survey. This can be limiting—the number of questions will probably be small, and open-ended questions may be excluded—but still may provide some good basic information about library use patterns and user needs.

If program planners choose to administer a library survey, they face a real challenge. Sample questions can be drawn from numerous library user surveys, so deciding what questions to ask is the least of the difficulties. Survey researchers use very exacting methods to achieve statistically valid results. If a survey is going to play a later role in campaigning for funds, it might be worthwhile to set up a valid, scientific study. Local students or faculty may act as consultants in the job. There are also numerous written materials on the topic, for example, *Basic Research Methods for Librarians* by Ron Powell (Ablex Publishing, 1991). Such aids can make a daunting task much more manageable.

A question that arises early on is whom to survey. Surveying everyone can result in very interesting data, illustrating, for example, some valuable comparisons across demographic groups. It will also mean much more work in labeling and distributing surveys (not to mention the cost of postage if you need to use U.S. mail) and entering data. You might choose to survey only the target population, for example, all of the minority undergraduates. Depending on the size of the school and the minority population, this might be a more manageable task. If the student body numbers in the tens of thousands, a sample of the target population would be easier to handle, though care needs to be taken to assure that the sample is statistically valid if that is a goal.

Basic questions will include descriptive information about the respondents (e.g., sex, race, class in school, major), how and how often they use the library, how they do research, and what changes they perceive would be useful to them. For this last question you may need to provide some suggestions, for library patrons typically respond that everything in the library is fine and they can think of no other improvements. You may also want to know what kind of library or educational background they have, what their current library experiences are, what kind of library instruction would be useful, and their views on the role the library can play in promoting diversity. Other questions will be determined by local interest as well as time and money factors (remember that a long survey will cost more to mail and take longer to key into a database for statistical processing). A quick check of the literature on user surveys will provide a wide range of possible questions (see, for example, University of Texas, A3, A30; Lubans, 245–53).

Opinions of teaching faculty and possibly others with extensive student contact, such as academic counselors, should also be sought. Faculty and student surveys can have parallel questions for subsequent comparison. Questions for faculty may include basic descriptive information (department, rank, length of time at the institution) as well as how and how much they expect their students to use the library, how they think students should best learn about the library, what programs or services they would like to see in the library, and what special needs they perceive.

An increasingly popular method of surveying the opinions of library users is through focus groups. This method is extensively used in marketing research to determine the interests or opinions of consumers, and library users can be viewed as consumers of library service. Several small groups are set up for focused discussion on a designated topic. For example, several groups of seven or eight students can be assembled to discuss library reference services. Focus groups provide a good way to get detailed information. A trained library staff member or someone hired for the job monitors the discussion and helps to keep it on track. The session is often tape-recorded so that the discussion can be transcribed later. Otherwise a note-taker will also have to be present. If your campus has a business school, there may be students or faculty members who could assist in setting up groups and training staff for little or no charge. Carefully assembled groups can also be fairly representative of the campus as a whole.

This is a brief view of methods of determining the library needs of the community. Both needs assessment and research techniques will be explored in further detail in later chapters. The key is to assemble as much information about the student body and their educational experiences on campus as possible at this early stage of program planning.

PULLING IT ALL TOGETHER

The puzzle that makes up the picture of a community has many pieces. The more you know, the better you can decide where to go next, or if special programming is even appropriate at this time. The community analysis should help identify pockets of need, how the library is viewed on campus, and what direction special programming is taking elsewhere in the institution. The complete picture should give a good idea of what kind of program would fit best in your setting; for example, although the target for service is always ultimately the student, the library may determine that the best way to meet student needs is to support special programs already in place.

Putting the pieces together should be an interesting exercise. Elements might be contradictory or seem incompatible. Some of the information may be simply wrong. But the more you get, the clearer the picture. Even if information is identified as incorrect, knowing the views of others— for example, that the black student group leaders believe that there are no special support programs when in fact there are—is valuable in and of itself. These resources can provide the snapshot information, the raw data, that go into the finished picture of the community. They can also help answer questions about the possible needs of that community.

With the pieces in place the picture should become clearer, but perhaps may also be more complex. The portrait of the student body will probably be the most detailed, since it is the target of the proposed service. Charts, graphs, or tables may make the picture easier to visualize and show the relationships between elements. Writing up a summary of the community analysis will also help to consolidate information. Such a summary need not be lengthy, or even include analysis. It would simply put the factual information in one place for easier access and clarification. You may find a wall chart or other visual devices for recording information useful for keeping the facts organized.

Looking at all the pieces together may give some idea of the institution's values and philosophy, particularly if the institution has a statement of goals. Another indicator of institutional values is where resources are concentrated. For example, if computers and technological development are what is hot on campus, a library program might concentrate on computer literacy for at-risk students. If national prominence is important to the school's administration, the library could point to the pace-setting nature of multicultural initiatives. Making the most of this abstract information can help the library develop a program more likely to be well-received on campus.

One way to get a handle on part of this abstract information is by using a model for institutional assessment developed by Bailey Jackson and Evangelina Holvino (1988). Their model, which can be used to evaluate the library or the entire educational institution, identifies four basic elements of a multicultural organization: promoting social and cultural representation by diverse groups; valuing and utilizing differences brought to the institution by diverse groups; eliminating racism and sexism; and accepting the validity of diverse claims on the organization's mission.

Jackson and Holvino identify three levels of multiculturalism within an organization. The levels and the stages within them are outlined below:

Level I. The Monocultural Organization

Stage 1: The organization strives to maintain the dominance of one group over others on the basis of cultural or personal characteristics (such as race).

Stage 2: The organization is not explicit in expressing the goal of maintaining the status quo, but in practice does retain the structure described in Stage 1.

Level II. The Nondiscriminating Organization

Stage 3: The organization removes discriminatory practices and hires minorities and women (mostly at the bottom of the structure), but does not change the corporate structure or basic culture. "Token" women and minorities at higher levels must fit into traditional practices.

Stage 4: The organization actively recruits and promotes women and minorities and openly addresses issues of discrimination of all oppressed groups. The organization remains committed to conforming to the norms of the majority.

Level III. The Multicultural Organization

Stage 5: The organization explores alternative organizational systems or structures to include and empower all members.

Stage 6: The organization includes members of diverse social and cultural groups as full participants at all levels and reflects the contributions of all groups in the organizational mission. The organization is committed to eradicating social oppression within its own structure and also acts on a sense of social responsibility to expand the multicultural ideology.

This continuum can give an institution a sense of where it is in becoming multicultural and what needs to be done to achieve a truly multicultural organization.

CONCLUSIONS

Librarians are often enthusiastic researchers, and might enjoy spending considerable time creating a thorough community analysis. Putting it together, however, is time- and resource-consuming. Despite the research expertise of librarians, not all of the pieces may be present. Time or resources may not be available to retrieve all relevant information. And some information may simply be unobtainable. It is important to set priorities, getting the most relevant information first, assembling as much additional data as possible, and extrapolating where necessary. Determining what is relevant will depend in part on the institution and on early program ideas.

The community analysis is an animated picture. What is true this year may not be true next year. Probably the most detailed analysis will be conducted at the outset of program planning. Nevertheless, as new information becomes available, the picture should be redrawn. Occasionally, program organizers may wish to revisit the community analysis even after the program is well-established. The community analysis is a first step in program planning. Once you know what you will be working with, then the fun begins!

REFERENCES

Evans, Charles. "A History of Community Analysis in American Librarianship." *Library Trends* 24, no. 3 (January 1976), 441–55.

Goldhor, Herbert. "Community Analysis for the Public Library." *Illinois Libraries* 62, no. 4 (April 1980), 296–302.

Jackson, Bailey, and Evangelina Holvino. *Multicultural Organization Development*. PCMA Working Paper #11; CRSO Working Paper #356. Ann Arbor: University of Michigan, Center for Research on Social Organization, 1988.

Lubans, John, Jr. "Evaluating Library-User Education Programs." In *Educating the Library User*. Edited by John Lubans, Jr. New York: Bowker, 1977.

Porter, Oscar F. *Undergraduate Completion and Persistence at Four-Year Colleges and Universities: Detailed Findings*. Washington, D.C.: National Institute of Independent Colleges and Universities, 1990.

Solmon, Lewis, and Tamara Wingard. "The Changing Demographics: Problems and Opportunities." In *The Racial Crisis in American Higher Education*. Edited by Philip G. Altbach and Kofi Lomotey. Albany: State University of New York Press, 1991.

University of Texas at Austin. General Libraries. *Comprehensive Program of User Education for the General Libraries*. Austin: University of Texas at Austin, General Libraries, 1977.

3

The Politics of Program Development

Theoretically, a good idea should sell itself. In today's financially hard-pressed and politically sensitive academic environment, the reality is that implementing even great ideas requires an astute assessment of where support is likely to be found and a carefully planned and timed strategy. You must be prepared to communicate clearly the nature and value of an outreach program, delineate clear, realistic, and measurable program goals, and justify resource allocation. Further, collaboration with appropriate individuals and departments is essential to building the support and communication network necessary to reach students and establish a vested interest in the library's program success. Equally important is the recognition that each institution has a myriad of attitudes, biases, interests, traditions, protocols, conflicts, and interconnections unique to it. Failure to assess and consider these subtle frameworks and how they might affect your efforts will leave you unprepared for the range of reactions and behaviors you will encounter, from apathy and misunderstanding to outright hostility. Even more frustrating will be the enthusiastic endorsements from people who lack any real power in the institution in terms of influence or resource allocation to be of help to you. Doubly problematic is the obstacle presented by lack of support or interest from the one department or administrator that could be essential to such a program's success. It is a serious mistake to assume that because multiculturalism has gotten great attention on your campus, with apparently a universal mission to address the needs of minority students, that everyone with a commitment to this agenda will be supportive of the library's efforts in this regard. You may be competing for resources from the same source or may simply be seen as an unwanted intrusion on protected "turf."

The specific steps involved in planning a program in the context of political realities include identifying groups and individuals necessary for program success as well as those factors likely to present obstacles, identifying sources of power and resources appropriate to your program, and planning an effective strategy to exploit these resources. (See the model presented in Table 3.1.) Crucial to this process is a fundamental understanding of your institutional culture and the complex factors that will contribute to the success of your program or provide obstacles to it. Understanding institutional culture does not empower you to change that culture—such change is extraordinarily difficult—but it will help you work more effectively within that culture by predicting how people are likely to react and behave, thus guiding your choice of strategies.

"THE INVISIBLE TAPESTRY"

Culture in higher education has been defined as "the collective, mutually shaping patterns of norms, values, practices, beliefs, and assumptions that guide the behavior of individuals and groups in an institute of higher education and provide a frame of reference within which to interpret the meaning of events and actions on and off campus" (Kuh and Whit, 12). Institutional cultures are complex, particularly in large, nonhomogeneous academic institutions, but the following elements in analysis will help provide a portrait of your particular college or university. They can be applied with equal value both to the library as an organization and to the larger institution.

Values and Goals

Does your institution have a strongly held and universally shared value system and agree on mission and institutional goals? If so, your work will be made much easier if you frame your program description in the context of this value system. Campus-wide commitments to improving the quality of the undergraduate experience, or to recruitment and retention of minority students and faculty, for example, provide powerful frameworks and clear-cut rhetoric to articulate your program goals and objectives. Remember that an essential part of establishing any program is education, and be prepared for faculty, students, and administrators who may not understand what you hope to accomplish unless

Table 3.1
An Analysis Model for Program Development

- Establish program goals and objectives
- Analyze the institutional culture to determine:

     what methods of approach appear to work successfully

     where the pitfalls may lie
- Identify on-campus individuals, departments or organizations that address

  the needs of minority students including:

     recruitment

     financial aid

     housing

     academic support

     social support
- Identify potential sources for program financial support both within and

  outside the institution
- Identify potential "positive agents" for program development

     institutional factors in your favor

     individuals, departments or organizations with whom you have worked

        successfully before, share values, or are engaged in endeavors that

        will profit from yours
- Identify obstacles to program development

     tensions and conflicts within the institution

     lack of resources
- Identify who can and likely will make decisions about the program

you can communicate the concept in terms of an agenda that is already important to them. On the other hand, if there is strong intra-institutional conflict or ambivalence over values and goals, you will have to assess carefully where institutional support for the program is likely to be found and at the same time identify potential intersections between your program goals and those of other sectors on campus.

Institutional Self-Perception

What image does your institution hold of itself? Do faculty and students pride themselves on high academic reputation? The diversity of the student body? Innovative curriculum? Long and hallowed tradition? In a recent commencement address at the American University's School of Law, the dean noted with pride, and the graduates heartily affirmed, the school's reputation as the "friendly" law school where support, not cutthroat competition, carried the day! Understanding what makes members of the academic community take pride in their institution will help you identify implicit values often far more reflective of the institutional culture than official mission statements or strategic planning documents.

Institutional "Personality"

Like people, colleges and universities have their own personalities. Would you characterize your institutional environment as competitive, power and status conscious, protective of turf? Or is cooperation valued and collaboration encouraged? Is the atmosphere laid back, thoughtful, cordial, and relatively conflict-free, or, alternatively, highly charged, pressured, confrontational, and aggressive? In organizations where accountability is high, failures are penalized, and people are overtly conscious that they are participating in a zero-sum game of approval and resource acquisition, you may find them to be disinclined to take risks, anxious about change, and afraid to experiment. Rather than appreciating the services your program can provide and the needs it might address, they may perceive it as a threat to their power and capable of diverting resources and attention from their own efforts. Conversely, in an atmosphere of trust and cooperation, individuals and departments will feel their efforts strengthened and extended by complementary initiatives. They will be much more willing to lend support and encouragement in shared endeavors to meet student needs.

Interactive Style

How do members of your academic community interact with each other, either in groups or as individuals? Are the interactions typically formal or informal? Campuses where the president meets informally with students for Sunday afternoon conversation and coffee in the residence halls are very different from large, hierarchical organizations where student groups must get on the president's calendar weeks in advance to discuss an issue. On smaller campuses, faculty, students, and administrators may routinely see each other daily, transacting most "business" on a one-to-one basis, eschewing the paper blizzard, dueling calendars, and telephone tag that characterize interactions on larger campuses. Size alone is not a determining factor. Electronic mail has established a new form of communication outside of established hierarchies, often extremely spontaneous and informal in nature. The important thing is to determine whether your quest for program support, financial and otherwise, is best initiated by talking with appropriate individuals on an informal basis or preparing a meticulously crafted, well-documented written proposal and sending it to your immediate supervisor. Further, as you are in the actual process of program building, the interactive style on your campus should influence your strategy for ongoing communication.

Organizational Structure

Understanding the structure of your institution goes beyond a mere review of the organization chart. You may have a vice-president for academic services, a vice-president for student services, and a vice-president for minority affairs. If you are planning to approach the administration for funding, ideally you want to contact the person who is likely to be most responsive to your program initiative and is in the position which appears to have the primary responsibility and authority to provide such support. Needless to say, the individual with the most enthusiasm for your program may not correspond to the appropriate institutional position. You also need to inventory carefully the departments and positions within whose purview such a student-support program falls. Is there an office for minority student services? What about links with housing, curriculum committees within schools and colleges, or key academic departments? Is there an Afro-American Studies program or a Latino Studies program? It is important to determine in what office and by whom, traditionally, such matters are addressed regardless of where the organization chart suggests they should be addressed, and also to identify people who will act as advocates and facilitators for your program development. Within the library, for example, you might logically take your program idea to the associate director for public services. What do you do, however, if in fact the library director has been outspoken in support for library services to minority students, while the associate director is lukewarm on this subject? You recognize that the library director has the authority and the value system to encourage your program development efforts, but that hierarchically you would propose the idea through your boss.

Decisionmaking

How are decisions made at your institution? Is decisionmaking highly centralized or decentralized? Is your program proposal likely to be referred to an internal library committee for review and assessment, or does the library director have the latitude, inclination, and resources to authorize your proceeding? Is there a faculty committee or council that advises the library, and can you expect that any new proposal would first be reviewed with them? Is decisionmaking generally by consensus, with a great deal of preliminary and open review, or are decisions made independently and unilaterally by key individuals both within and outside the library? Is student input sought before decisions affecting them are made? Are standing committees, councils, and so on, logical parts of the decision-making process, or are ad-hoc groups likely to be appointed? Do you have the authority to divert resources and attention to the program, or is any activity along these lines subject to the approval and funding of the institutional administration?

Leadership

What kind of leadership does your library have? The institution as a whole? Can you expect strong support and guidance from your library director or from the dean for academic services? Is your leadership visionary, placing value on innovation, creativity, and entrepreneurship, and willing to let staff experiment and make mistakes, or, alternatively, conservative and averse to taking risks? If active support is not immediately forthcoming, does the leadership style nonetheless foster and support individual initiatives and encourage collaboration with other units? Do both library and institutional leaders support multicultural activities and programs? Is your library leadership respected within the campus community and likely to advocate your initiative effectively, or will you be expected or allowed to fill that role?

Tensions

What tensions exist within the library and on campus? Is the relationship of students and faculty with the administration cooperative or adversarial? On large, research-oriented campuses the perennial tensions between research and teaching will affect the support, time, and interest faculty may be prepared to give to your outreach effort. Is the library competing for space with other departments? If a debate is raging at your institution over core curriculum, or if the institution is confronting declining enrollment, such tensions may undercut understanding and receptivity for your program. Administrators tend to focus their attention on the most immediate problems; if drained of energy and worn down with confrontation, they may be disinclined to perceive the importance of your program unless it is readily apparent that it will contribute to the campus good on a value system they understand.

Now that you have a clearer picture of how people and groups on your campus and within the library are likely to react to your program development efforts, it is time to map out a strategy for program development that includes identifying and obtaining necessary resources.

SOUND STRATEGIES FOR PROGRAM DEVELOPMENT

The essence of timing and hierarchy—whom do you talk to first? To their chagrin, most librarians have discovered at one time or another that they had a great idea or did something with the best intentions that unexpectedly made any number of people angry. Your first task is to convince those to whom you are accountable that this program is a good idea and to gain their support and advocacy. If you have a library director who values innovations and is committed to diversity, willing to support experiments and to carve out or reallocate resources to support new initiatives, and has the time and inclination to discuss your ideas in depth, you are in ideal circumstances. It is just as likely, however, that you will have to approach a supervisor unfamiliar with the rationale behind such an outreach program, beset by competing needs for resources, and of necessity extremely selective about what projects or programs to advocate with an equally beleaguered administration. Regardless of how receptive your supervisor is likely to be, taking the following steps can never damage your case:

- Make sure that you are well informed and pull together any material you consider key to the issues. This might include copies of an institutional mission statement related to undergraduate education, minority student recruitment, multiculturalism, and so on, and any literature or information on similar programs or initiatives at other institutions.

- While your supervisor or library director assuredly does not want to be surprised by hearing about your idea from other members of the staff or from faculty before hearing about it from you, he/she will appreciate some initial evidence of perceived need on the part of students and faculty for such a program. Talking with minority students about how they perceive the library and what their needs are as well as with faculty and staff who work with students will give you a clearer picture of the degree of understanding and enthusiasm the library will encounter.

- Make a list of the units on campus you are likely to be working with and note those you have an existing relation with on which you can likely draw. If there are key individuals and departments with whom you have never made contact, it is important to note that too. Be sure to have a clear picture of areas your program might replicate, and be prepared to identify turf both within the library and outside on which you may be intruding. Thus you will anticipate related questions that an administrator is likely to pose and demonstrate that you have given consideration to pertinent issues.

- Have a clear estimate of needed resources and what resources at your disposal you are prepared to commit. The two fundamental principles about money on today's campuses are, first, that there is simply not enough to do all the desirable and important things that need to be done, and second, that a capable administrator generally can and does find the resources to do the things he/she really believes are important, even if that means sacrificing something else. Determine the following:

  1. What amount of *your* time are you prepared to commit, and what will you be giving up?
  2. What are the implications of this shift in your priorities?
  3. If you have staff to allocate to program development, what percentage of their time and effort are you prepared to commit, at what expense, and with what impact?
  4. What, if any, funding sources exist within the library or elsewhere on campus for new initiatives? Is there a fund to support initiatives to improve undergraduate education? Has the institution earmarked money to be used for minority student support programs or to match funding for new minority faculty positions?

These considerations will demonstrate your understanding of the budget realities on your campus and that you are prepared to work in committed partnership in supporting the program.

THE LARGER CONTEXT—MAXIMIZING ADVOCACY AND MINIMIZING CONCERN

Now that you have your supervisor's support and have provided the ammunition for him/her to act as an informed advocate for you where necessary, you need to plan a strategy for simultaneously building support within the library and on campus. Keeping in mind what you know about both the current institutional climate and the underlying institutional culture, review the list of relevant individuals, departments, and organizations. Since you want to build support and momentum for the program, first contact those that fit the following criteria:

- The library is in good standing with them and has worked successfully with them before.
- There is some history of personal relationship, that is, if you know someone well in the admissions office but not in academic counseling, start there.
- They are likely to be helpful in suggesting contacts and persuasive approaches or identifying sensitive issues across the campus.

With the feedback and input you get, in short order you must begin contact with less familiar sectors of the campus. Keeping in mind what questions or concerns they are likely to have will prepare you to deal with them. In general, people will want to know:

- what exactly this program is;
- what it has to do with them and how it can help them;
- what you expect from them or are likely to expect;
- why it is important;
- what your overall program goal is, stated as succinctly as possible;
- why the library is involved—remember that information literacy, the increasingly technological information environment, outreach, and so on, mean something to you, but may not be obvious or important to someone else.

In your discussion, focus on collaboration and avoid demands that might be perceived as impositions on their time or resources. Listen more than you talk, and watch carefully for signals like boredom, wariness, or confusion. Be very careful about making excessive claims, and be honest about the unknowns you are wrestling with. Make clear that their perspective is crucial to your evolving vision of the program. Be prepared to pursue an idea and make a necessary commitment if the signals are there, but avoid pressing people too hard. On initial contacts a polite and interested reception may lay a perfectly adequate groundwork for subsequent involvement—don't spoil it by overstaying your welcome or being overly aggressive about nailing down the immediate next steps. Your single greatest allies are your own belief in what you are doing and your commitment to students. A sincere enthusiasm can come across powerfully. Knowing that you do not need to manipulate people or carry them along on the wave of your natural charisma or forceful personality is likely to make you feel much more comfortable.

This kind of interaction can be very subtle, and that is why it is so important to have an understanding of institutional culture as well as some preliminary knowledge of an individual's personality or how a group generally responds. Some people and groups are open and informal in style; with them it is perfectly appropriate, and indeed highly effective, to meet and discuss the program in an open-ended way without presenting a formal proposal or asking for any kind of commitment. Much can be gained in this kind of interpersonal give and take. Under other circumstances, such casual use of an individual's or a group's time would be perceived as naive on your part and would violate unwritten protocols of communication. In this situation, forwarding a program description clearly spelling out the above points is the better strategy.

CRACKING THE "TOUGH NUT"

It is realistic to expect reactions ranging from sheer lack of interest to outright hostility. In your zeal, it may be tempting to conclude that resistance or antagonism reflects lack of vision, lack of concern for minority students (or students in general), or a thinly disguised attempt to preserve a decaying social order. The actual causes are, of course, far more complex, and people's reactions are probably grounded at least in part in legitimate concerns and may stem from perceptions that have nothing to do with the program itself. If you can identify the source of concern, you will be well on the way to dealing with it. Consider the following possibilities:

- *Lack of understanding*. Be prepared to devote considerable time to educating people about what you are trying to accomplish. They may have no conception of what the library does or can do for students and no familiarity with the problems students encounter in the library. The use of students as peer advisors may be a novel idea to them, and they may have no conceptual framework in which to place the program.

- *Competition for resources.* If you get money for something, chances are someone else will not. Ironically, even on campuses committed to minority student support initiatives, this money is finite, and chances are that everyone else on campus is trying to advance the institutional goals in this area. This is a fact of life, but you can mitigate concern somewhat if you can make people see that the resources you get will somehow benefit them directly, or work out a collaborative effort so that you both get resources.

- *Competition for approval within the institutional value system.* Since resources often follow perceived value, groups and individuals may feel that you are intruding on their closely protected turf or diverting attention from their efforts. Every organization has people who begrudge recognition given to others. One way to deal with this is to make them partners who share to some extent the recognition the program receives.

- *Difference in philosophy.* It would be a mistake not to recognize that affirmative action, multiculturalism in curriculum and library collections, and even the best model for staffing a reference desk are under considerable debate on campuses today. The controversy is likely to spill over, resulting in critical scrutiny of any endeavor by the library or anyone else in these areas. You will have critics, but recognize that you will have many allies as well. Rather than expecting to find a way to resolve the issue, accept that such discourse is part of the academic environment.

- *Past history.* Your prospects may be affected by frustrations or angers stemming from something the library did in the past. If an earlier collaboration with a department failed miserably, the department may harbor residual resentment or be skeptical that the library will follow through reliably. If an administrator who returned an overdue book was poorly treated by a staff member, your first exchange with them may involve letting them express their irritation and trying to alleviate it in some way. If perceptions of the library, for whatever reason, are extremely negative on campus, reconsider whether this is strategically a good time to start a new program. New initiatives are probably a lower priority for the library than improving basic services, unless your program has the potential to improve the image of the library as a whole.

ENLISTING THE SUPPORT OF COLLEAGUES AND STAFF

The general dynamics and issues within your library are unlikely to be dramatically different from those on the campus as a whole, and you need to approach your colleagues and staff with the same consideration you give the larger institution. One additional concern is, however, likely to be paramount for each staff member: What additional work will this make for me, and how will it affect my job? You cannot assume that your staff are yours to allocate indiscriminantly to this program even if you have the authority to do so. Similarly, even if the library director is prepared to direct the participation of your colleagues, you have little to gain by forced cooperation. Even staff members enthusiastic about the program may be reluctant to sacrifice their current activities or may fail to perceive that it has anything to do with them. Establishing a peer outreach program means investing considerable time and commitment in recruiting, training, developing, and supporting the students who will serve as staff. It also requires an accepted vision that undergraduates are capable of working in partnership with experienced professionals and, in fact, admitting that there are things professionals can learn from students in providing public service to other students. Factors likely to enhance staff support and acceptance include:

- prior positive experience in employing students in positions of public service responsibility;
- a preexisting model of reference desk staffing that has routinely included staff who are not librarians;
- previous experience with innovative or experimental program or service initiatives;
- a library environment with open communication where it is acceptable to discuss problems and issues related to a complex endeavor and where people who raise concerns or point out problems are not labeled negative;
- leadership that encourages and staff who value working in a team approach.

If these factors are absent in part or in total, you must be prepared to devote considerable time to educating and persuading staff and colleagues through the same analysis of the library subculture and with the same strategies used to approach the library leadership. Understanding, cooperation, and support from your staff and colleagues are essential.

IDENTIFYING RESOURCES

Regardless of how you decide to structure your program and on what scale you implement it, staff and materials must be allocated specifically for program support. In general, funding comes from four potential sources:

1. reallocation of staff/money from your own budget;

2. reallocation of staff/money from within the library budget as a whole;
3. additional funds from campus sources;
4. additional funds from external sources.

Identifying resource possibilities in the above order is particularly useful framed in the larger context of sound program development. Your willingness and ability to divert tangible resources within your purview will contribute significantly to convincing administrators, whether within or outside the library, of your commitment and your ability to plan realistically. Additionally, in an environment where money is tight, there may be few or no sources of funding on which to draw, regardless of the level of enthusiasm the program engenders. The following considerations should also be taken into account in planning a strategy for funding:

- Planning program development in established phases, making it possible to seek "seed money" to get the program off the ground and use a subsequent program review to justify additional and ongoing support.

- Identifying likely sources of new money and submitting a proposal for program funding for a specified length of time.

- Considering the two facets of program support—how to get the program off the ground and how to pay for it on a permanent basis. Funding for the first circumstance can come from a variety of sources. In order to accomplish the second, permanent additions to or reallocations within the library's base budget are required.

In examining possibilities within your budget, consider the following possibilities in diversion of resources. Can funds be diverted from other activities? If you have an hourly budget for additional support for staffing the reference desk, can some portion of that be used to hire student counselors? Have activities declined or changed in some areas (reserve use or technical processing, for example), permitting reallocation of some hourly money attached to those areas? In the same vein, is there an open position that could be earmarked for a program coordinator, or could money in the base budget be used to support hourly staff? Alan Dyson (1989) describes using just this strategy to create a position of diversity librarian at UC-Santa Cruz. If a head of reference or other staff position is normally responsible for new public service program planning, is it reasonable to expect that some portion of that individual's time could be devoted to program development? Is it equally reasonable to expect that staff time could be devoted to shared training efforts? A certain amount of creativity and brainstorming can contribute greatly to identifying possible resources, but it is equally important as you develop your budget to keep in mind that these are real resources with a dollar value attached to them. It is not crass, but rather sensible as well as politic, to include specifically in any proposal you bring forward the nature and amount of reallocated and "contributed" library resources. This is essential for a complete picture of what the program actually costs (crucial in any program development effort), but also essential in making the case for the library's level of commitment. It is also an effective strategy for establishing a program cost-sharing model in which program support is shared in some way by both the library and an external funding source.

Additional Library Resources

Does your library have funds set aside for new initiatives and, if so, is this money for special projects? Money for the initial program development or for the first two years is an excellent start, but you must have a strategy already identified and articulated to support the program after that. Similarly, perhaps the library has earmarked money specifically for diversity-related initiatives, for example, recruitment of minority librarians, that might serve as a source of initial or ongoing funding. If the library has an existing grant related to developing programs or services for minority students or for undergraduate initiatives, that might also be a source of partial funding for an aspect of the program. What about other units within the library which may be developing programs or services for graduate students or minority faculty? Collaborating across the library system in identifying overlapping program components and shared goals is one way to argue more persuasively for funding. Does the library have an active friends group, endowments, or gift money that could be tapped for program support? Might residency programs, field experience, or internship programs provide possible staff support for the initial stages of program development?

Possible Sources on Campus

In identifying possible sources of funding, the campus portrait you assembled when analyzing institutional climate and culture will be invaluable. Before approaching anyone, it is important to consider such tangible indications that the unit or individual is likely to be receptive to your request as institutional mission statements, strategic plans for individual units, and so on. With the many developing concerns and agendas in academic institutions today, the following can serve as a checklist for relevant possibilities:

- new initiative funds for undergraduate education, minority student support, or programs to extend multiculturalism in the campus environment;
- administrators in relevant positions likely to have discretionary funds available to fund new programs: the vice-president for student services, the dean for student affairs, the office of minority students services or minority affairs, for example;
- resources available from such units as Housing, Financial Aid, or schools, colleges, or departments with whom the library has established programs. Financial Aid, for example might be able to target a certain number of work-study positions to encourage student interest and employment in the program, resulting in considerable real-dollar savings in personnel costs.

Possible Grant Sources

While externally funded grants may seem like the obvious answer to a dearth of new institutional money for program initiatives, the prospects for grant funding are bleak in the current library environment. Based on feedback from other academic librarians throughout the country, it appears that such programs are generally supported by internal reallocation or development funds made available from within the institution itself.

CONCLUSIONS

Regardless of where the funding possibilities lie, a sound strategy for financial support includes a carefully framed proposal with clearly articulated program goals, a method for program evaluation, a program description, and a complete budget. Fundamental to this process is a clear understanding and representation of what you expect to accomplish. Establishing realistic, measurable, and relevant program goals tied directly to the overall mission of the library and the larger institution is essential not only to gaining the required understanding and support on campus but to ensuring that the vision underlying the program initiative is one shared by all concerned.

REFERENCES

Dyson, Alan. "Reaching Out for Outreach: A University Library Develops a New Position to Serve the School's Multicultural Students." *American Libraries*, November 1989, 952–54.

Kuh, George D., and Elizabeth J. Whit. *The Invisible Tapestry: Culture in American Colleges and Universities*. ASHE-ERIC Higher Education Reports, 1988.

4

Establishing a Program Budget

The first step in identifying total program costs is to delineate program support components, including staff, ongoing operating expenses, and any associated capital costs for program start-up. It is important to recognize hidden as well as obvious resources devoted to the program, since any evaluation or program justification will generally be expected to include a program cost analysis. Administrators will want to have a clear picture of total program costs, including those that are contributed or reallocated. You will also avoid unpleasant surprises later on in finding that unexpected expenses or campus-wide personnel cuts, for example, place your program in jeopardy. Therefore, even if you plan to devote a portion of your current staff to the program, use existing equipment or facilities, or absorb supply costs within a current budget, include all such costs in your program budget. If you are preparing a proposal asking for even a portion of extra support money, no part will be scrutinized with greater detail than the budget page. Keep in mind, however, that your program can be as basic or extensive as you choose based on the resources available. Also, there are many ways to keep costs modest. The program cost depends directly on *what* you plan to do, and on what *scale*.

Before beginning to assess needed resources and attendant costs, determine the following:

1. *What is the size of the initial targeted population?* Be realistic about the first year of the program and what you can accomplish. Possibilities include targeting first-year minority students, first- and second-year minority students, all new incoming minority students (including trans-

fer students), or all undergraduates. The number of students you hope to reach will determine how many peer counselors will realistically be needed to reach those students. The targeted population number will also affect publicity costs such as mailings and printing.

2. *How many student counselors are you going to have?* The number of counselors will directly affect the amount of time required for supervision, training, mentoring, and recruiting and will determine the percentage of time a position will have to be devoted to these activities. Since the counselors will generally be enrolled students themselves, it is unrealistic to expect them to work more than 10 to 15 hours per week. If you determine that you would like to begin with having peer counselors at your reference desk or available in the library 40 hours per week, you will need three or four students for this level of staffing.

3. *How will your academic calendar affect staffing?* If your institution has a limited enrollment during the summer, you might elect to confine activities to the busiest academic terms. On the other hand, if the library expects to participate heavily in a summer orientation program, you might decide that it is important to deploy staff and activities throughout the calendar year appropriately. Examine the academic calendar, totaling the number of weeks you expect to have student counselors engaged in activities (including the time they will spend in training), and determine the average number of hours each week the counselors will work. This will give you a basis for the total number of student hours per year.

4. *How will this program be supervised?* Depending on the program scale, overall program direction can take all or part of a professional position. Estimate the amount of time the various coordinating and public service activities will take each week in order to determine the percentage appointment (or percentage of a full-time equivalent).

5. *What salary/hourly rates are involved?* After deciding on an appropriate level for a supervisory position (either existing or to be hired), determine the salary level involved and establish a suitable hourly rate for student assistants if different from the standard rate in the library. The scope of job responsibilities peer counselors will undertake may argue for a higher level of pay. (See Chapter Five.) This rate should be worked out in consultation with the appropriate personnel office. Identify the standard overhead (or staff benefit) rate used at your institution for each position category. Overhead includes all indirect costs above salary, including staff benefits such as leaves, unemployment compensation, retirement, health and dental benefits, and so on. Since even hourly staff are usually eligible for some benefits (for example, if they incur on-the-job injuries), an

overhead figure considerably less than that for full-time staff is generally included. This cost must be factored into your personnel budget.

6. *What specific program activities do you expect to engage in during the year?* Making a list of the general program elements will help identify where you will incur specific costs and help you fashion activities within your resources. A single reception for 1,000 students could be very expensive or inexpensive depending on the lavishness of your entertaining. A single flyer distributed through an on-campus mailing or in residence halls, on the other hand, is a very inexpensive way to reach students. If there are existing newsletters, electronic bulletin boards, or regularly scheduled events of which you could take advantage, costs in reaching the campus may be very modest outside of the staff time involved. This is an area of great flexibility. If you have limited or nonexistent access to public microcomputing facilities and no equipment budget, you have two options: devise a sound strategy and proposal for acquiring such equipment, or concentrate your user instruction efforts in other areas.

STEP 1: DETERMINING WHAT THE PROGRAM WILL COST

The following elements are basic to an outreach program:

- personnel
- supplies
- start-up costs (equipment purchases, furniture, space renovation, telephone line installation, logo design, etc.)
- operating expenses (monthly telephone charges, postage, publicity, travel, computer software, graphics design, equipment repair, printing, photocopying, etc.)

Personnel

Staffing includes the person responsible for overseeing the program, the peer counselors, and any other personnel required for program support on an ongoing basis. If the program coordination is going to be handled by a librarian as a portion of current duties or a reworked position, determine the realistic percentage of time to be devoted to program implementation and supervision. Also determine whether this percentage might change in subsequent stages of the program.

Hourly staff costs depend on the number of peer counselors, the number of hours each student works per week, the appropriate hourly rate attached to each position, and the level of staffing during portions of the academic year. Be sure to include overhead costs related to staff when figuring the budget. (See Figure 4.1.)

Figure 4.1
Estimating Hourly Staff Costs

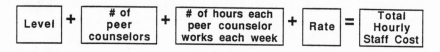

Supplies

Computer paper, mailing envelopes, folders, letterhead, posters, name tags, promotional items, food for receptions or other program-related events—these can add up significantly over a year, especially if you plan to reach a large number of students. After mapping out the nature and extent of program activities, estimate the resources likely to be required. For example, if you plan to send a program newsletter to 3,000 students twice a year and a program brochure to 4,000 incoming students each year, you can quickly calculate the paper and printing costs involved. Be realistic not only about necessary costs but about the level of funding available. It may not be possible to build all the elements you would like into the first year, so be prepared to live within your means without sacrificing program visibility.

Start-Up Costs

Consider what will be needed in terms of office space, desks, chairs, telephones, file cabinets, and so on, and determine whether they are currently available or can be assembled from existing resources. If the program coordinator is an existing position (or portion thereof), additional space and furniture may be needed only for the counselors themselves. If the peer counselors are working primarily at the reference desk, in an existing microcomputer center, or regularly out in other facilities around the campus, a separate office may not be required. Try to determine if the counselors will have adequate access to computer workstations for their training and skill development and whether they are expected to work solely with the online catalog or to provide assistance in other computer applications. Additional equipment may include a telephone answering machine, display case, or bulletin board. Even if the library has a logo suitable for use with program materials, a one-time expense for a newsletter masthead or a well-designed program brochure may be worthwhile. Consider if one-time costs can be spread over the first two or three years of the program. Table 4.1 suggests some possible program components with cost estimates.

Table 4.1
Selected Budget Items: Cost Estimates

The following table lists a number of common program support elements with accompanying cost estimates. These costs may be helpful in putting together very rough preliminary budget figures, but clearly could vary significantly depending on local or institutional service costs, volume of item purchased, institutional salary levels, etc. (Volumes were based on a target population of 1400 minority undergraduates and a total target undergraduate population of 10,000.)

NUMBER	ITEM	COST
4,000	Brochures (2-color, color-separated, camera-ready copy)	$ 800
3,000	Newsletters (11x17, folded, 2-color, camera-ready copy)	$ 360
10,000	Letterhead paper (1-color)	$ 350
1,000	Posters (including $500 graphic design fee)	$ 1,500
2	Advertisements (student newspaper, 1/4 page)	$ 800
	Reception with food for 200 students	$ 250
	Promotional Items	
100	Tee-shirts (camera-ready copy, 3 color @ $6.50 + $50 set-up cost)	$ 700
1,000	Buttons (camera ready copy, 1 color)	$ 275
1,200	Pens (imprinted)	$ 400
1,200	Pencils (imprinted)	$ 300
	Staff	
	Assistant Librarian annual salary	$26,000
	Student assistant hourly rate	$ 5.50

Operating Expenses

These will vary widely depending on what you plan to do, the resources available, and the size and nature of your institution. Postage costs, for example, will be considerably lower on campuses where the majority of undergraduates live in dormitories. Because the bulk of your mailing can be done through campus mail or distributed in student mailboxes, there will be no charge to the library. A good time-saver is to request mailing lists already in mailing-label format (if available) from the registrar's office or data systems office. There will generally be a charge for this service, so be sure to figure these costs into your budget. If the program coordinator or the peer counselors are expected to attend staff development programs or national or local conferences, set aside money for this unless there is a source of central funding for activities of this nature. Extensive promotional activities, especially if they involve campus newspaper or radio station ads, can be expensive, and you may opt for more cost-effective methods of communication. Keep in mind the need to update printed materials regularly and to upgrade software used in conjunction with the program.

STEP 2: PUTTING TOGETHER A BUDGET

Since the goal is to establish a permanent program, it is best to lay out a multiyear budget. This will allow a reasonable amount of time for ongoing program evaluation and reassessment, and will also delineate ongoing program costs as distinct from initial implementation costs. It also provides the option of establishing the program in phases, for example, beginning with four counselors in the first year and building to eight in the third year. If additional funding, in whole or in part, is being sought to develop the program initially with the expectation that the library will work toward internal reallocation to make the program operation part of the permanent base budget, this should be reflected in the budget projection. Two sample two-year program budgets follow: the first a modest-cost program assuming limited available resources, the second a more extensive program assuming the possibility of additional funding and the necessity for microcomputer workstations (see Tables 4.2 and 4.3). Budget II, for example, permits two newsletter mailings a year, substantial promotional activity, and higher staffing levels. Note that some costs can actually *decrease* in the second year if first-year expenses include online graphics design, several years' supply of support materials, or one-time equipment costs.

Table 4.2
Program Budget I

YEAR 1

Personnel

Program Coordinator (Assistant Librarian) - .5 FTE	$	13,000
Staff benefits @ 24%	$	3,120
Hourly staff (4 student counselors) - 1152 hours @ $5.50	$	6,336
Overhead @ 8%	$	506
Total	$	22,962

Non-personnel

Supplies	$	500
Operating expenses	$	500
Total	$	1,000
Total	**$**	**23,962**

YEAR 2

Personnel

Program Coordinator (Assistant Librarian) - .5 FTE	$	13,650
Staff benefits @ 24%	$	3,276
Hourly staff (6 student counselors) - 1728 hours @ $5.50	$	9,504
Overhead @ 8%	$	760
Total	$	27,190

Non-personnel

Supplies	$	500
Operating expenses	$	500
Total	$	1,000
Total	**$**	**28,190**

Table 4.3
Program Budget II

YEAR 1

Personnel

Program Coordinator (Assistant Librarian) - 1 FTE		$ 26,000
Staff benefits @ 24%		$ 6,240
Hourly staff (6 student counselors) - 1728 hours @ $5.50		$ 9,504
Overhead @ 8%		$ 760
	Total	$ 42,504

Non-personnel

Supplies		$ 1,500
Operating expenses		$ 2,500
Equipment		
1 Mac SE 30 + laserwriter		$ 3,000
Telephone answering machine		$ 150
Software		$ 300
	Total	$ 7,450

	Total	**$ 49,954**

YEAR 2

Personnel

Program Coordinator (Assistant Librarian) - 1 FTE		$ 27,300
Staff benefits @ 24%		$ 6,552
Hourly staff (8 student counselors) - 2304 hours @ $5.50		$ 12,672
Overhead @ 8%		$ 1,014
	Total	$ 47,538

Non-personnel

Supplies		$ 1,500
Operating expenses		$ 1,000
Equipment		
Lobby display system		$ 500
	Total	$ 3,000

	Total	**$ 50,538**

REFERENCES

Shields, Gerald R., and J. Gordon Burke, comps. *Budgeting for Accountability in Libraries: A Selection of Readings.* Metuchen, N.J.: Scarecrow, 1974.
Trumpeter, Margo C., and Richard S. Rourds. *Basic Budgeting Practices for Librarians.* Chicago: American Library Association, 1985.

5

Developing a Staff

One of the most important responsibilities of beginning a new peer information counseling program will be interviewing, hiring, training, and retaining a strong staff of student assistants.

DEVELOPING A POSITION DESCRIPTION

Once the goals and objectives of the peer assistance program have been determined, the next step is to create a description of the student workers' duties. The format of student position descriptions generally resembles that of regular full-time staff position descriptions, with a few significant differences, such as noting specific hours to be worked. Begin with a position title and a brief description of the program, explaining its goals, responsibilities, and requirements.

Some large research libraries have a central personnel office that issues standard student position forms. More formal job description forms might be posted in other units around campus to attract potential employees (Minority Student Services, Office of Minority Affairs, Academic Advising, etc.). Figure 5.1 is an example of a peer information counseling student position posting.

Tasks and Duties

It is important to list clearly in the position description all the major tasks, duties, and responsibilities of the job. Students need to know the

Figure 5.1
Peer Counselor Position Description

Position Title: Peer Information Counselor

Position Description: Peer Information Counseling (PIC) is an outreach program for students of color. PIC is located in the Undergraduate Library, and its goals include making all students (especially students of color) better able to utilize the library's rich resources. PIC students are responsible for staffing the Undergraduate Library's reference desk and the Academic Resource Center.

Responsibilities:

- Helping to answer patrons' questions at the UGL reference desk.
- Helping patrons use the online catalog and indexes.
- Teaching patrons how to use the library's resources.
- Teaching patrons how to use word processing software on a Zenith or Macintosh computer.
- Assisting program coordinator with a variety to special projects including putting together displays, writing bibliographies, handouts and flyers, assisting with special teaching projects.
- Assisting with the future planning of PIC activities.

Skills/Abilities:

Required: A strong public service attitude, sophomore standing, flexible schedule, ability to work well with others, ability to work at a busy public service desk, strong communication skills. Some computer use. Ability to make a one-year commitment to Peer Information Counseling program.

Desired: Some familiarity with the Library's online catalog, some familiarity with Microsoft word. Previous experience working with the public. Knowledge of the library and campus.

---

major responsibilities up front to help them decide whether to apply for the job and to help them ask probing questions during the interview. Details of how the tasks and duties are to be performed can be explained in the job interview.

Required Abilities vs. Desired Abilities

It is important to distinguish between skills and abilities deemed absolutely essential for peer assistants to possess and those that are merely desirable. For example, it is more important for students to be able to interact with the public in a pleasant manner than to possess specific library skills. The latter can be acquired during training. This will increase and strengthen your pool of applicants and make for more diverse recruiting.

When writing the position description keep in mind that student assistants can only be expected to function as support personnel; they are students first, employees second. This is not to say that expectations of their performance within this framework should be low. However, students cannot be expected to perform the same duties with the same commitment as full-time salaried employees.

When writing a position description, consider the following:

- How much time will you have to train the student assistants? If you have little time to devote to initial and ongoing training, then the skills and traits you require of applicants must be noted more specifically. Keep in mind that this will significantly decrease the size and diversity of your candidate pool. It will also lessen the benefits of the job for the students who apply.

- What is reasonable to expect of student assistants based on how much training you will give them and what you will be paying them?

- With what skills do you expect the student assistants to enter the job? Is it reasonable to expect them to speak three languages and be computer-literate if you are paying them $4.50 an hour?

- Will you allow your student assistants to work at a public service point by themselves? This places a great deal of responsibility on the student; is this reasonable given your library setting and staff configuration?

- What hours would you like the student assistants to work? If specific hours or ranges of hours are not posted, at least give a general idea of the time of day and the number of hours per week expected of the student.

RECRUITING STUDENTS

Once you have written the position description, you are ready to begin recruiting peer assistants. Several methods of recruiting eager and committed students should be considered. Most supervisors will want to combine a number of methods, formal and informal, to get the most diverse pool of applicants possible.

Formal Methods

Formal methods of recruiting students include printed materials that make use of existing venues. They allow you to spread a broad net across campus in order to attract a large pool of candidates.

1. *Personnel notices.* Most campuses have many places where job notices can be placed. The most common include student services buildings and offices that handle student financial aid, central personnel hiring, minority student services, and so on. Usually your library or central personal office will help you to determine which spots to include on your posting list.

2. *Newsletter articles.* In order to publicize your program, you may want to issue a newsletter several times a year. Including a small recruitment notice in the winter semester newsletter is a great way to get the word out about available jobs. If you can procure from the registrar's office a mailing list of undergraduate students whom you may want to target (students of color, students living in campus residence halls, etc.), you can mail the newsletter directly to those students. This always produces a great response from a self-selected, motivated audience.

3. *Publicity on campus.* Posting flyers, posters, and notices on bulletin boards in campus buildings frequented by students is also a good way to recruit students. Some departments require that the flyers be approved before they will post them; many allow anyone to post a flyer without approval. You can either arrange for a student to post the flyers around campus (make a list of where you want them posted; take a tour of the campus ahead of time to make your list exclusive), or you can mail the flyers to various campus units, asking them to post them for you. The latter method is somewhat risky; some units may not take the time to post your flyer. Some likely places to post position announcements include:

- any minority student services unit. At the University of Michigan several offices fall under this category, including the Office of Minority Affairs, Minority Student Services, the Comprehensive Studies Program Office (summer bridge and retention office), etc.

- minority student organizations. Most campuses have student-run organization offices located in a central spot on campus. At the University of Michigan these offices are located in the campus Union and include the Black Student Union; Socially Active Latino Student Association; Minority Music, Theater and Dance Students Association; Society of Minority Engineering Students; Native American Student Association; Asian American Association; etc. Each one of these organizations has potential students for your program; their members tend to be more tuned in to the campus and more concerned with helping others.

- organizations for minority faculty and staff. Often faculty and staff of color have strong relationships with their students of color.

- academic units that have strong minority student enrollments. At the University of Michigan the Communications Department, American Culture Department, Women's Studies Department, and Afro-American and African Studies Department all have good minority representation.

4. *Recruiting from other library units.* If your library is part of a multilibrary system, put out the word that you are recruiting to all library units on campus. In the smaller units there may be librarians who have contact with students who want to work. Other units cannot always give students all the hours they want, so a split between units is often possible. Smaller libraries may not be happy to give up their trained students entirely, but if the benefits of the program are explained to the supervisors, they may be more willing to share their students.

5. *Direct mail.* If your campus registrar will allow access to mailing lists (permission may be needed from the appropriate administrator), mailing out a full position description to targeted students may result in an overwhelming response.

Informal Methods

The role of informal methods cannot be underestimated when trying to recruit students. Often these methods attract excellent students through personal references from colleagues and other students.

1. *Use of the campus network.* Through your campus network of friends and colleagues you will often find that they have contact with many excellent students. Putting the word out casually or through a memorandum that you are actively recruiting students lets them know that they can make referrals to you. These students will be coming to you with the recommendation of someone you trust.

2. *The replace-yourself method.* Another good way to find student workers is through students who already work for the library. Attaching a note to timecards or asking students you know and admire for names of other interested students will often result in quality applicants. Once you have a group of students trained and working for you, you have a built-in source of new names. (Jokingly, Peer Information Counselors are told that in order to leave the program, they must find a replacement. Although they know we are being facetious, this method has provided PIC with many excellent students.)

MARKETING THE JOB

Advantages of Becoming a Peer Counselor

You will want to attract the largest pool of applicants possible in order to get top-quality students. In order to attract a large number of students, you must be able to convey the advantages of the position to potential applicants. Some of these advantages include:

1. *Gaining research skills.* Many students do not make good use of the library's resources. If you can convince them that they will have valuable and marketable skills at the end of their tenure with you, and get paid for them to boot, then the position becomes much more salable.

2. *Computer literacy.* Stress the interaction they will have with an online catalog, developing computer searching skills, and CD-ROM skills. Microcomputing experience using different software packages is also an advantage. These skills are very marketable to future employers. Make certain the applicants know this.

3. *People skills.* Communication skills are important in any job. Your students will be able to polish and build on their communication skills. They will learn to communicate with all types of people (both patrons and colleagues) in their tenure with the library.

4. *Getting to know resources and librarians.* Working in the library is beneficial for students no matter what their major. At the University of Michigan, peer advisors have majored in science and engineering, English, psychology, political science, premed, prelaw, and business. All have benefited from improved research skills and from learning to use the indexes, reference sources, and online catalog, even though some rarely had to write formal papers. These research skills make them more aware of the range of information available, more information-literate, and ultimately more employable when they graduate.

5. *Working in a pleasant atmosphere.* Working in the library is a lot nicer than flipping burgers at a fast food joint and more interesting than most student jobs at the college or university. Most libraries are climate controlled and people oriented, making them nice places to be employed.

6. *Helping people to solve problems.* Who doesn't like using their expertise to help people solve problems? Once students have a little experience assisting patrons with a variety of questions, they develop a strong sense of confidence and pride in their abilities.

7. *Flexible schedule.* If this is an option for your students, publicize it in the job description and in the interview. Most good students have a very tight schedule, with classes, extracurricular activities, and social lives competing for their time. If they can work out a schedule that fits into their busy lives, they will be much happier with the job.

8. *Having important input into program development.* Employees are happier if they feel they have some vested interest in the outcome of their work. Also, students may help you see things from the perspective of those you will be serving, which may lead to new ideas. During the interview give candidates examples of how student ideas have been used in the past, or discuss how you intend to use student input in the future.

9. *Project work: writing experience, self-directed and teamwork opportunities.* The use of student assistants to put together exhibits, write promotional flyers, and compile bibliographies on subjects of interest to them is another selling point of a diverse job. In the interview find out if the student would enjoy these responsibilities. Project work has the added benefit of not having to be strictly scheduled; students can easily work it into their schedules.

10. *Varied responsibilities.* If students know that they will not be doing the same old thing day after day, they will be much more responsive to the position. Stress that working with the public is never the same on any two days, and give examples of varied requests and questions that have passed by the reference desk or other service points.

INTERVIEWING

An interview is a nerve-racking experience even for veteran employees, so expect the students you interview to be somewhat uneasy. To allay their discomfort, set a relaxed mood before you begin the formal part of the interview. Perhaps a short tour of the work area or a quick exchange about an informal topic will set students at ease, enabling them to concentrate on answering the interview questions to the best of their ability.

1. *Questions that should and should not be asked.* Just as when interviewing for a full-time position, certain questions should and should not be asked. Questions relating to marital status and religious beliefs should not be asked. Try to ask questions that will evoke more than a yes or no answer. Areas to cover in a standard student interview include the following:

a. Ask about the applicant's job experience. What relevant work experience does the student possess? Many seemingly irrelevant experiences may in fact give you clues to the student's past performance. For instance, a student employed by a groundskeeping company may have gotten experience working in a group or individually against a deadline.

   • What did they like about their past jobs, and what did they dislike?

   • How did they deal with the parts of the job they disliked? (Every job has parts that are disliked by the worker, so it is important to learn how they deal with these stresses.)

   • Did they work with the public?

b. Ask about the applicant's ability to work with the public. If students have worked with the public, there are certain things you will want to know about their interaction style and communication skills.

   • Did they ever deal with difficult people in their past job?

   • Ask them to give an example of a difficult encounter, and how they handled the situation.

   • What do they like about working with the public?

   • How would they characterize their oral and written communication skills?

   • How do they react to being a role model for other students? Especially minority students?

c. Ask about the applicant's ability to work in a busy environment. Most libraries are very busy places. For some people this can be distressing, for others it is exciting. It is best to see how the student feels about this environment during the interview. Furthermore, a public service point is often very busy one minute, then very quiet the next, which requires shifting gears often. Find out how the student feels about this as well.

   • Can the student juggle working with the public while working on an independent special project between busy times?

   • Can the student remain approachable to the public even if his or her special projects are often interrupted?

   • Does the student get frazzled when several people are making demands at the same time? (Phone-in patrons often compete with in-person patrons at the same time.)

d. Will the student have a work-study grant? If your unit is strapped for funding, you may want to consider this as one of your hiring criteria. If work-study is an important issue, put it in the job description or register the position only at the college work-study office. It is always best to ask during the interview if the student does have work-study, because many students do not really understand the significance of this to employers.

2. *Explain the basics of the program.* Illustrate for the student how the peer program fits into the overall mission of the library and the university. Explain the premise the program was built on, the program's basic goals and objectives, and why it is felt the program will make a difference. Above all, explain why their role is very important to the overall success of the program.

3. *Explain the basics of the job.* During the interview it is always a good idea to give the interviewee an idea of what the position will be like. Describe what a typical shift will be like and some of the tasks they can expect to encounter. This helps students make a much more informed choice about whether or not they wish to work for the library.

4. *Explain the dress code.* Basic policies such as dress code are best brought up during the interview. This is the time to inform the student of the way the library does business. If the applicant has a problem with the dress code, then you know you don't have a match.

5. *Explain the kind of commitment expected.* Stress that the library will rely on them tremendously. Although one cannot reasonably expect as much commitment from an hourly employee (who is a student first and an employee second) as from a full-time employee, certain standards must be established.

- They must believe in the goals of the program or they will not understand the importance of what they are doing.
- They must understand that they are relied upon to report for their shifts.
- They must understand that the way they treat patrons affects the success of the program, the library, and the people served.
- They must understand that without them, the student employees, there is no program.

6. *Make certain you have answered all their questions and give them the opportunity to add comments.* Always remember to give them the option to call you later with further questions. Give them your business card or your name and phone number to facilitate further contact. Likewise, take their name, number, and address so that you can contact them.

Get their local as well as permanent or summer address in case you must contact them after the school year is finished.

7. *Make certain the hours fit their schedule.* If students will be working through the lunch or dinner hour, or late at night, ask if they will be able to make arrangements to eat or to get home safely. They must be comfortable with the hours you have to offer.

MAKING THE DECISION TO HIRE OR NOT TO HIRE

Hiring the staff for your peer information program will be one of the most important steps in getting it up and running. The quality of student staff will determine how successful the program ultimately will be. Chose staff very carefully, just as you would for a full-time position. There are a few standard things to consider when the interviews are over and hiring decisions must be made.

1. *Attitude of the applicant.* Was the student attentive during the interview? Did the student give full answers to the questions, or short, distracted answers? Why was the student interested in the job? Is the student genuinely interested in helping others? Did the student display curiosity during the interview? Did he or she ask questions about the job? All these questions can help predict the on-the-job attitude of a future staff member.

2. *Previous experience with the public.* Did the student have any other relevant experience working with the public? Even if the job was as a cashier at a fast food restaurant, what they said about that experience could be a very important indicator of how they would interact with library users.

3. *Class schedule.* Is the student's class schedule flexible enough to accommodate several blocks of time to work? Scheduling students to work for less than 90 minutes at a time is seldom beneficial to the library or to them.

TRAINING

Creating handbooks for student employees or using existing ones to lay out rules and regulations and training is suggested. See Appendix One for the student handbook from the Undergraduate Library at the University of Michigan.

1. *Training for the reference or information desk.* Having a well-thought-out training plan saves a lot of time and overlap in the long run. Create a multistep plan to cover the basics of working on the reference desk, then supplement the initial training with ongoing sessions once counselors have a bit of experience working with users. The ongoing

training sessions can be held at weekly, biweekly, or monthly staff meetings.

At the University of Michigan, a multistep training program has been developed for all hourly reference workers. (See Appendix One for more comprehensive details of the training program.) The basics of this training program include sessions covering the following:

- Introduction to the Undergraduate Library (approximately 2 hours):
    1. UGL's function as a teaching library (library's philosophy)
    2. Basics for all student employees:
        a. Timekeeping functions
        b. Student Employee Handbook (see Appendix One)
        c. Setting up a schedule for remaining training sessions
    3. Tours of UGL and Graduate Library
- Orientation to the Reference Desk (approximately 2 hours):
    1. Reference desk review of drawers, bins, files, etc.
    2. Commonly asked questions
    3. Emergency procedures
- Access to the Collection (approximately 2.5 hours):
    1. Known item searches (books and serials)
    2. Unknown item searches (books and serials)
    3. Online catalog training
- Reference Interview and Search Strategy (approximately 2 hours):
    1. Examples of patrons' questions that illustrate why careful reference interview is necessary
    2. Search strategy, including background, books, and current information
- Basic Reference Tools (approximately 2 hours):
    1. Fact tools vs. finding tools
    2. Run through the reference stacks and index tables
- Automated Services (approximately 2 hours):
    1. CD-ROM products
    2. Online search procedures

2. *Training for computing center functions.* If peer counselors will have computer training responsibilities as well as reference responsibilities, a training session to cover the basics of how to use word processing software must be held as well. Even students who know how to use the software should go through the training, because they will learn not only the mechanics of how to use the software, but also how to teach a basic software session to other students who may be computer phobic to some degree.

At the University of Michigan, Microsoft Word is the word processing software taught in the Academic Resource Center (ARC). ARC is a small computing and study site located on the second floor of the Undergraduate Library. Peer Information students staff this site, assisting people who have made appointments and walk-ins who ask for word processing tutoring.

In the basic word processing training session the peer counselors are taught:

- How to put at ease a patron who may be computer phobic. Patrons who have never used computers before are probably going to have some fear of using a word processor. Setting a relaxed, comfortable mood is very important.
- How to format a data disk. At ARC all patrons tutored are given a free data disk with the phone number of the Peer Information Counseling program stamped on it to remind them of the program's services.
- How to boot up the program disk.
- How to open a file on the data disk.
- How to move around within a data file. Included in this segment are the basics: how to set margins and tabs; how to use the cursor; typing, inserting, and deleting text.
- How to save the file.
- How to print the file.
- How to exit the file and close the software.

Only the basics are stressed because it is best not to overload the patron during this brief 30- to 60-minute introductory session.

3. *Ongoing training/staff meetings.* Once staff have completed the initial introductory training sessions, ongoing training and regular staff meetings are important to keep them informed of changes and to impart more detailed information to them on a regular basis. Once they have worked a few hours on the reference desk they will be better prepared to accept more detailed training because they will have a relevant context in which to place the added knowledge.

At the University of Michigan, Peer Information Counselors meet with their supervisor once a week the first few months of the new academic year, then once every two weeks later in the year for extra training and staff meetings. Some of the extra training sessions include:

- How to find materials on racial and ethnic minorities.
- How to handle problematic patrons and incidents in the library.
- How to find statistics on any topic.

- How to find information in political science.
- How to find literary reviews and critical works on any given author.
- How to find information in the sciences.
- How to find biographical information.

(For detailed training plans on all of these topics, see Appendix One.)

4. *Policies and procedures.* At some point in the ongoing training process you will want to make sure that students have read the policies and procedures manual for the reference department. This includes dress code, policy on finding substitutes, how to answer the telephone, and so on. You will also want to make sure they have read their student manual and the emergency procedures manual as well. Students are always well-intentioned but sometimes fail to follow through when they are busy. Give them paid time to read these materials, then double-check to make sure they have done it.

5. *Training pitfalls.* Along the long, intense training road, there are a few pitfalls to watch for. Some include:

- Different ability levels on entering the program. Some students may enter the program with extensive online catalog knowledge and strong knowledge of the way the library functions, while others may not even know how to read a Library of Congress call number. You will have to fold all ability levels into this training. A good way to keep the more knowledgeable students interested in the training sessions is to involve them in the teaching. Having them assist with training the less advanced students will strengthen their already strong skills and help them recognize where they need more training as well.

- Students not asking questions. Always recognize that anyone, not just students, may be afraid to ask questions before they get to know you (or whoever is conducting the training). If students are not asking questions during the sessions, try to anticipate which areas may be confusing to them, and tell them about questions you had when you were learning that section. This way they will realize that they are not being slow, that the material is genuinely confusing, and that they should not be shy to speak up. Encourage them to ask questions throughout the training sessions. When they do ask questions, never become impatient. One negative incident may warn the others that their questions will not be welcomed by their supervisor.

- Training overload. Early in the semester it is very tempting to try to jam in as much training as possible. It is recommended that formal training not exceed six hours per week or two hours per session; otherwise you risk overloading your students. The amount of detail that students are able to absorb is significantly reduced after this amount of time, so when covering the material, watch for signs of inattentiveness; it may be time to quit for the day! You may wish to consider having them observe interactions at the reference desk once they have reached this threshold.

- Scheduling training sessions so everyone can attend. Finding a time when everyone can get together for training will be one of your greatest challenges. Sessions may have to be scheduled early in the morning or late in the afternoon to accommodate everyone's schedule. It is much better to train at odd times than to have to schedule several times for the same session.

6. *Creating a comfortable learning environment.* Making sure that the students are relaxed and comfortable will pay off in the long run. Providing snacks before the session begins will give them an extra bit of energy and aid concentration. Also, making sure they are comfortable asking questions is very important. Make sure they know you don't expect them to remember every little detail of the training session. Once they realize that their on-the-job experience will reinforce the details as they progress, they will be able to relax and enjoy the training.

7. *Training effectiveness and assessment: exercises.* Along the training path you may wish to reinforce and test the effectiveness of the material taught in the training sessions by assigning information exercises. (See Appendix One for exercises.) When you hand out the exercises, specify when you want them returned. When they are returned, promptly check them. If some individuals have problems with the exercises, schedule a separate training session for them to reinforce the concepts.

At the end of the first semester you may wish to survey the students to determine if they thought the training was sufficient, if they were overloaded, and so on. Ask them for suggestions on how to improve the training.

8. *Encouraging students to ask questions of any staff members they work with.* Once the formal training is over, encourage the students to use their co-workers as resources. Stress to all staff members that they should also be encouraging the students they work with to ask questions.

9. *Use of observation during training.* As part of the initial training period each student should be scheduled to observe several hours per week at the reference desk. This is where the real learning will take place; the concepts in the training session will be strongly reinforced during these times at the desk. Encourage the students to follow their co-workers into the stacks, over to the online catalog terminals, anywhere they go to assist patrons. It is nice to have special "in training" or "observer" badges printed up for the students to wear while they are

observing; that way, patrons do not ask them questions before they feel ready to begin answering them.

POLICIES AND PROCEDURES

When beginning a new student assistant program, certain policy and procedural issues should be considered. Once decisions have been made about these issues, the policies should be documented. Some of these issues may include:

1. *Finding substitutes for vacations, changes in schedules, etc.* Depending on how many student assistants are hired, you may wish to consider asking them to make their own substitutions when their schedules need adjusting or when they want to take a day off. This will save the coordinator a lot of time and worry. This policy must be firmly established at the beginning of the hiring process so that the students understand their responsibility at the outset.

2. *Dress code.* A decision must be made early on how strict the student dress code will be. Should the code mirror the full-time staff dress code? Should it reflect more relaxed standards, since most students do not have a professional wardrobe? At the University of Michigan, a few basic standards of dress for working at the reference desk include no shorts, no ripped clothing, and no Spandex clothing. Students should be encouraged to dress in a manner that signals to the public that they are responsible, approachable individuals.

3. *Standards of behavior.* Policies on friends visiting at the desk, professional ethics of discussing patrons at the desk, reading or doing homework at the desk, and so on, all must be considered. Students need to be told orally or in written form what the standards are at the beginning of employment.

4. *Personal use of library equipment.* Again, students need to know if they will be allowed to use staff equipment on off-hours for their own projects or enjoyment. A balance needs to be struck between providing perks for student employees and keeping equipment available to employees on duty.

- Telephones: Should students be allowed to use the office phones (not at the reference desk, of course) for local calls? If they are allowed to make personal calls, what restrictions should apply to length and number of calls? What is the potential for abuse of this privilege? An explanation of the parameters of use at the beginning of employment should be sufficient to ensure against abuse of this privilege.

- Computing equipment: This is a wonderful employee privilege if it can be provided. Students need to know at the outset what the parameters of use are. It must be strictly understood that students using the computing equipment must not interrupt job-related work by others.

- Staff areas (lounge, offices, etc.): Perhaps the easiest privilege to offer students is the use of staff lounge facilities for lunch, dinner, study breaks, etc. Rules as to whether they will be allowed to bring nonemployee friends to the staff areas should be established. Whether or not they will be allowed to use the staff refrigerator, microwave, utensils, etc. (if they exist), should be explained. Using offices for non-work-related activities may be a bit stickier. Offices are usually kept locked, which means keys must be made or kept on hand in a safe place.

5. *Difficult or abusive patrons.* Students need to know what is expected of them in situations where they encounter difficult or even abusive patrons. They need to know how far they should go in assisting a patron who is difficult before referring that patron to a full-time staff member. They need to know the procedure for calling security in cases where there are no full-time employees in the building when patrons are threatening or abusive.

6. *Food and drink policy.* Students need to know why food and drink are not allowed in most libraries. They need to know about preservation issues. They need to know if there are areas in the library where they can bring food or drink. This information should be conveyed in terms of what is expected of employees and what is expected of patrons. Student employees should be told at the outset if they will be expected to police food and drink usage of patrons within the library.

7. *Emergency procedures.* Every library should have a concise emergency procedures manual. Students should be paid to read the emergency procedures manual. Then the protocol for what is expected of them while working at the reference desk or in other areas of the library under the program's direction should be explained. This should be reviewed each semester.

MENTORING

Perhaps one of the trickiest topics to discuss is how to mentor employees in their jobs. Students look to their colleagues, supervisors, professors, and academic advisors, among others, while they are in school. They are at an uncertain point in their lives, not knowing whether they will have jobs when they graduate, whether they will have enough financial aid to continue their programs, and so on. They need to know that the people around them care about them as individuals rather than just working hands. Although much of mentoring involves the use of intuitive skills, a few principles are common to every good mentoring experience:

* Be available. When students need to talk about their job or personal issues, their supervisor must make them feel welcome and cared for. This means always being available, no matter how busy you are. Your employees are the most important part of your job; they will make or break your programs, goals, and every other part of your responsibilities. They should be given first priority in terms of your time. If the students sense that your time is too precious or that you are always rushed, they will not come to you with problems, questions, or even suggestions.

* Be aware of what is going on on campus that affects your students outside the workplace. It is in your best interests to keep up with student publications on campus. Finding out, for example, that distribution of student financial aid has been delayed or that a student in your peer assistant's residence hall has died may impact on your students' ability to function on the job and in their classes. Find out how your students are dealing with problems and issues that concern them. They will know that you care about their success, not just in the workplace, but in their personal lives as well. If you initiate such dialogs, they will become more comfortable initiating conversations in the future.

* Learn about your students: their families, future plans, classes they are taking, exams, papers, etc. Take a little bit of time each day to ask students about their lives outside of the workplace. You will develop a better sense of them as people, and they will realize that you are a caring person.

* Make sure they know you care (you need to know they care too—a relationship is a two-way street). Asking them about their lives shows you care about them, and sharing some of your life shows them you trust them as well. Students who take an interest in you as a person, and not just as a supervisor, will make an extra effort to fulfill your goals for the program.

PERFORMANCE EVALUATION

To evaluate work, you need to keep a set of standards or goals in mind. Setting performance goals or standards is an important responsibility that must be considered before the hiring process begins. Performance goals and standards help students understand what will be expected of them and how they will be evaluated on the job. Several methods, both formal and informal, can be used to evaluate students' performance.

Formal Evaluation

Formal methods of evaluation involve observations that are recorded for future use. The student should be aware that you are conducting the evaluation and know how the evaluation will be used. Formal evaluation may be conducted by the student, by peers, or by librarians.

- *Self-evaluation*. Once each semester it is a good idea to have each student fill out a self-evaluation form (see Figure 5.2). This is a good way to find out what areas students perceive they need to strengthen. After receiving the completed self-evaluation form, the supervisor should meet with the student individually to discuss areas that need to be strengthened, and develop an ongoing training plan to develop those areas. Other areas of strength should be emphasized and praised as well. It should be noted that self-evaluation often is more critical than outside evaluation, and strengths should be emphasized in the post-observation meeting. If there is a pattern of perceived weaknesses on the part of several of the peer counselors, it is a good idea to bring this up at a staff meeting after having spoken to each student individually. A staff meeting may be devoted to strengthening their joint understanding of the problematic area.

- *Peer evaluation*. To ease the pressure of conducting evaluation sessions, and to get the student perspective on other students' work, peer evaluation is a valuable tool for testing performance. It should be noted that most peers are reluctant to give poor evaluations to one another; however, constructive criticism is often provided by this method. Having peers observe each other's work while at the reference desk using a standard performance evaluation form (see Figure 5.3) can give the supervisor a valuable second perspective.

- *Evaluation by a librarian*. Performance evaluation by librarians or other full-time reference staff is a valuable way to test expertise at a higher level than that of self- or peer evaluation. It is more expensive to use librarians to actually conduct the evaluative process. However, it may not need to be done as often as the peer evaluations or self-evaluations.

Formal performance evaluation should take place at least once a year for fully trained students, and perhaps once a semester for newer students so that they can learn from their evaluations.

Hold a brief conference with each student to discuss their performance after the evaluations have been turned in. A discussion of students' strengths, as well as areas that may need improving, should take place. Be careful not to be too negative. This may be the very first time these students have been evaluated at a job, and they may feel somewhat vulnerable for that reason. Mixing praise with points that need to be strengthened will

Figure 5.2
Self-Observation Form

Name: _____   Date: _____

Preparation for Work:

Appearance appropriate?	yes	no	eventually
Name tag on?	yes	no	eventually
Ready work area if necessary?	yes	no	eventually
Read reference log?	yes	no	eventually

	Need to strengthen	Feeling competent
Acknowledge patrons promptly?	_____	_____
Good eye contact?	_____	_____
Ask probing questions In person? On the phone?	 _____ _____	 _____ _____
Sensitive to special needs such as language or physical difficulties?	_____	_____
Does the patron know I expect her/him to participate, such as stay or follow me?	_____	_____
Maintain appropriate feedback with patron In person? On the phone?	 _____ _____	 _____ _____
Make efforts, when appropriate, to teach and encourage independent activity?	_____	_____
Knowledgeable about Periodical indexes? Electronic tools? Reference books?	 _____ _____ _____	 _____ _____ _____
Make accurate, careful, appropriate referrals?	_____	_____
Offer opportunity for patrons to ask more questions?	_____	_____
Encourage patron to return for future needs?	_____	_____
Watch for signs of confusion and follow up if need be?	_____	_____

Figure 5.2 (continued)

Notes/examples:

	Need to strengthen	Feeling competent
General evaluation:		
Alert for patron needs?	_____	_____
Ready to help colleagues?	_____	_____
Follow up on questions with colleagues to get better answer?	_____	_____
When time permits, practice proactive reference?	_____	_____
Aware of basic ethical considerations?	_____	_____

Notes/examples:

Summary:
Am I
polite?	_____	_____
thorough?	_____	_____
collegial?	_____	_____
independent?	_____	_____
service oriented?	_____	_____

Do I
have a good rate of speech?	_____	_____
have good eye contact?	_____	_____
teach when appropriate?	_____	_____

Notes/examples:

Notes on observation circumstances such as time of day, desk busy, time of term, etc.

Figure 5.3
PIC Staff Observation Form

Name: _____   Observer: _____

Date: _____

Preparation for Work:

Appearance appropriate?	yes	no	eventually
Name tag on?	yes	no	eventually
Read reference log?	yes	no	eventually

Comments/Examples:

Reference Interview:	Good *needs more experience*	Excellent
Acknowledge patrons promptly?		
Good eye contact?		
Polite and encouraging manner: In person?		
On the phone?		
Sensitive to any special patron needs such as language or physical difficulties?		
Maintain appropriate feedback with patron to be sure information need is being met: In person?		
On the phone?		
Make efforts, when appropriate, to teach and encourage independent activity on the part of the patron?		
Knowledgeable about: Periodical indexes?		
Electronic tools?		
Make accurate, appropriate and careful referrals?		
Offer opportunity for patron to ask further questions?		
Encourage patron to return for future needs?		
Watch to be sure patron is not confused by directions and follows up with further assistance if needed?		

Comments/Examples:

Figure 5.3 (continued)

General Evaluation:	Good needs to strengthen	Excellent
Alert for needs of patrons?		
Ready to help colleagues?		
Follow up on questions with colleagues (such as asking for advice even after the patron has left).		
When time permits, practice "proactive" reference? (For example, moving to busy service points when the desk is quiet; alert for confused-looking patrons.)		
Aware of basic ethical considerations (such as not discussing patrons publicly)?		

Comments/Examples:

Summary:	Good needs to strengthen	Excellent
Is the reference staff member:		
Polite?		
Friendly?		
Thorough?		
Knowledgeable?		
Collegial?		
Independent?		
Service oriented?		
Does the reference staff member:		
Have good speech rate?		
Have good eye contact?		
Teach when appropriate?		

Comments/Examples:

help assure them that you appreciate their work and will help them to accept constructive criticism as well. Remember that areas that need strengthening may be indicative of poorly designed training. Ask students if they feel the training should be improved.

Informal Evaluation

Informal evaluation includes all evaluation methods that are continuous and not formally instituted. Students will not necessarily know that evaluation is taking place, because it has not been formally set up ahead of time. Some types of informal evaluation include:

- Working with them on the desk, correcting mistakes, and praising work. This can and should be done by all staff members who work with the peer counselors. When students make a mistake, they should be corrected as soon as possible, in a diplomatic way. The responsibility for correcting mistakes and praising correct answers and referrals lies with everyone because the supervisor cannot always be there when the problem or positive encounter occurs. If a problem is recurrent, the supervisor should be made aware of it. It is okay to correct behavior at the desk as long as it is done diplomatically and no one else is there. If the desk is busy, you may want to casually take the student aside, then or later, and explain the error.
- Correcting mistakes and behaviors without being discouraging or threatening. It is very threatening for a staff member to be corrected or reprimanded in any way. Students are often tougher on themselves than others are on them (judging from the self-, peer, and librarian evaluations they have undergone at the University of Michigan), so one must be careful when correcting behaviors. Begin correcting the student by accepting half the responsibility for the mistake; in this way the pressure is lifted off them, but they realize that the mistake has been made. One can do this by beginning the exchange, "Perhaps the training didn't really adequately cover this, but . . . ," or "I should have placed more emphasis on this earlier, however . . . ," etc. Remember to praise correct answers and behaviors as much as possible. When students are just learning, they are nervous and vulnerable in the public's eye. They need to hear they are doing a good job as much as they need to hear when they are wrong.

RETENTION OF STAFF

Retaining your staff is very important for many reasons. It is a huge advantage of keep your student staff for several years running for a number of reasons:

- The more experienced the staff, the higher quality the service they provide will be.
- Training time is decreased when experienced staff return from year to year.
- More experienced students can assist with training new students.
- Services can begin earlier in the school year when you have a significant portion of returning students.

Keeping a well-trained student staff does not require a magical touch. Treating students with respect and making them feel they are a vital part of the staff goes a long way in retaining them. Here are some easy ways of making your staff feel valued that may help with retention:

- Make sure they know the benefits they will receive from working at the library. Tie in their training, the questions they answer, and their development of a reference knowledge-base to their lives as students. Ask them about their classes, if they have to write papers, and about their assignments. Relate this to their reference work.
- Give them increased responsibilities as they grow in their job. Ask them to assist with training others, ask them to assist with planning the year's activities, etc.
- Gather input on program ideas and development from your peer counselors. Who is better in touch with the students' needs and feelings than their peers?
- Communicate library developments to them. When something changes let them know. This will help connect them with the "big picture" at the library.
- Tell them you appreciate their assistance, insights, and suggestions. Then show them you take them seriously by putting good ideas into action. A supervisor who delivers only bad news is soon looked upon negatively, as is the job. You want them to be pleased to come to work!
- Take an interest in your students as individuals. When they know you care about their success, they will trust you and go the extra distance for you. Ask them about classes, family, and friends.
- Encourage a sense of community among their peer counselors. They will more happily substitute for one another and help one another out when they are friends as well as colleagues. Host get-togethers several times a year where everyone can come together socially and have fun.
- Pay them as well as you can. It is far better to pay a decent wage and have select hours than to pay poorly and have lots of work coverage by disgruntled students. Pay fairly. If the library system sets an overall rate that does not reflect the expertise and training your students are expected to obtain, talk

with the library's personnel director to discuss ways in which the peer students' salaries may be raised.

* Provide perks if possible. Letting peer counselors use computers after hours, providing them with office space, or assisting them with research on their own papers are a few ways to make students feel they are special.

* Stay in close touch with their needs. Find out in which areas they feel they need added training. Watch to make sure they have not overcommitted themselves in terms of hours and special projects.

REFERENCES

Bluemel, Nancy Larson, and Rhonda Harris Taylor. "Saving Just One Student." *Book Report* 9 (January/February 1991), 36.

Childress, Schelley H. "Training of Student Assistants in College Libraries: Some Insights and Ideas." *Arkansas Libraries* 44 (March 1987), 25–27.

Fuller, F. Jay. "Evaluating Student Assistants as Library Employees." *C&RL News* 51, no. 1 (January 1990), 11–13.

MacAdam, Barbara, and Darlene Nichols. "Peer Information Counseling: An Academic Library Program for Minority Students." *Journal of Academic Librarianship* 15 (September 1989), 204–9.

Westbrook, Lynn. "Students and Support Staff on the Reference Desk." *C&RL News* 50, no. 9 (October 1989), 808–10.

Wilder, Stanley. "Library Jobs and Student Retention." *C&RL News* 51, no. 11 (December 1990), 1035–38.

6

Program and Service
Development

Program development is like marketing a new product: we examine and reexamine our potential market, we assess our resources, we cater to what is current, we make the most of our advantages. This approach may make some librarians uncomfortable; nevertheless, though the language and the activities may at times seem foreign, the process of developing new services requires salesmanship.

In developing programs and services librarians tend to rely on their observations at the reference desk and in other patron encounters to determine the need for library instruction or related services. If several people repeatedly ask for assistance in finding movie reviews of foreign films, for example, the librarian may track down the class for which the assignment is being done and try to convince the professor that a bibliographic instruction session is in order. Or library staff may respond to frequent requests for help in using *Psychological Abstracts* by producing a handout. This is the "response approach" to bibliographic instruction (Kirk, 89)—librarians wait and see what needs present themselves, then react.

The response approach certainly works and may be the only way some libraries with limited resources can help those who need it. The librarian can feel certain that what she provides will be used—the need has already been made clear. This method, fortunately, may miss a segment of the market by neglecting nonusers as well as those who do not ask when they have questions: "Special emphasis should be placed on the importance of actively seeking out students who appear to be having problems. Unless librarians . . . reach out and anticipate student needs and approach library patrons and offer to help, then the library remains a storehouse of books that only the most aggressive or knowledgeable students use effectively" (Kirk, 89).

Another approach to program development is to review the library literature. There is currently a groundswell of interest in the subject of multiculturalism and diversity in libraries. Articles, workshops, continuing education programs—many resources are available to inform librarians of new ideas and programs in this area. So much is going on that it might be difficult for a library just embarking on a program to identify what options will work best in its environment. Using the response approach and making the most of the body of professional information are important steps in getting a program up and running. Use of more systematic and aggressive approaches, however, might ultimately produce a beneficial product.

NEEDS ASSESSMENT

Why do a needs assessment? Needs assessment not only informs the planning process, but will also provide supporting evidence for program proposals. A needs assessment is a formal process to "determine and close the more important discrepancies between 'what is' and 'what should be'" (Newhouse, 33). Once the differences between the present and desired conditions are identified, a needs assessment will also help program planners to set priorities.

Needs assessment encourages two-way communication between the community and the library. Communication between the two is often limited to reference desk encounters, or mediated by others, such as via faculty descriptions of their expectations of students. Newhouse notes that "most communication failure between libraries and community patrons is [the] resolution of incorrect, or trivial, needs" (33). A formal needs assessment gives the library the opportunity to identify real needs from the perspective of the community and can lead to more meaningful programming.

Planning for Needs Assessment

Like any research process, needs assessment, to be most effective, should be carefully planned. First, clearly state the intended goals of the assessment. Determine who will play what role in the process, what resources are available to conduct the assessment, and what sources of information to use.

Goals. A primary goal of the needs assessment will naturally be to identify the library needs of the target constituency. Another obvious goal is to structure the base for the design of any new programming. The assessment may also need to play a third role if it is to be used as part of a proposal for financial support. To identify what methods will receive the most attention, determine who the audience will be for the final product. Will that audience prefer a scientific survey performed by an impartial technical expert, or letters and testimonials? An understanding of the needs of your audience will shape decisions about methods of assessment, sources of information, and final presentation.

Personnel. It is most likely that a library staff member will supervise the needs assessment and have primary responsibility for its implementation. Planners should consider including community members in the planning and implementation process. In a small institution it may be valuable to include prominent students and faculty members in the process. The community may be more likely to accept the final determinations of the assessment if they participated in some way in the planning process—for example, in proposing questions (Hobbs, 25).

Resources. Resources will include personnel as well as financial support for the needs assessment. It may be difficult to shake loose resources for this stage of program planning. It may help to remind those in control of the resources that a good needs assessment will provide the most solid base for an effective program.

Timeline. Newhouse (35) has suggested that a library needs assessment requires a period of twelve months. Realistically, few will have that much time to spend on this stage of program planning. In planning the needs assessment, set a timeline and deadline for completion. Of course, keep in mind the impact of the academic calendar on any attempt to get information from students and faculty! If time is very limited, choose a methodology that will allow at least some direct input from the community. They are the ones, after all, who will ultimately assess their own information needs.

Elements of Needs Assessment

The core issues a needs assessment seeks to discern are the following (Rothman and Gant, 36):

1. Who requires assistance, and what are the characteristics of the group? How many are there?
2. What is the type of problem? (For example, in the library, is it lack of research skills, lack of familiarity with computers, or discomfort with the

staff; or there may be a group that falls behind the rest of the community or behind some agreed upon standard). How serious or extensive is the problem?

3. How did the problem start, and how has it changed?

To answer these questions, the researcher will need to go to several sources. Librarian observations represent a critical component. Student input is also invaluable, although the library community has long recognized that patrons often do not know what kinds of services are possible, and therefore may not be able to identify what they would like the library to do for them. Faculty, staff and administrators, administrative documents, and other sources inform the assessment as well. A thorough needs assessment should include the following:

- *A community profile.* This would include students, faculty, administrators, and other service providers (such as academic counselors). The profile should describe the community—number of students, breakdown by class and program of study, ethnicity, sex, etc.—and also include information on their attitudes toward the library and their views toward library instruction and student need for such instruction. If at all possible it might be useful to assemble such a profile even before selecting a target group. The profile might help to identify the pockets of real need (for example, rather than targeting all minority students, it may be most appropriate to target minority freshmen—or all freshmen).

- *Courses.* Take a look at the range of courses offered on campus. In particular, are there courses required of all students? Are there courses or departments in which students of color or other targeted groups are heavily represented? In any program planning process these courses can be a springboard for ideas about what kind of library instruction students might need as well as sources of ideas for how to reach and appeal to students. If a large segment of a target group is in the English Department, for example, a peer counseling program might hire a number of English majors and create a program component on finding literary criticism. If the sciences are a more critical area, the program might feature a major component on finding scientific information.

- *Library staff observations.* In particular, those who work in reference departments are very likely to have impressions of the information needs of students. They are less likely to be able to break down those observations by class level, academic group, or ethnicity of students, since individual patron encounters tend to blend and overlap in memory; nor, of course, can they directly address the needs of the nonuser. Nevertheless, they are likely to be able to categorize areas of concern for students and put forward informed opinions about the potential needs of nonusers as well.

- *Literature review.* It is useful to get ideas from other libraries about their programs, how they determined the need, and what steps they took to remedy that need. In addition to or in place of a literature review, communicating with library staff at other institutions is another way to get this kind of information. State, regional, and national conferences allow the opportunity to make direct contact with colleagues. LOEX (Library Orientation Exchange) and similar information clearinghouses are another source of information. These clearinghouses are able to distribute examples of products, including survey instruments, statements of goals and objectives, program outlines or evaluations, and other documents from other libraries. Another means of communicating with other librarians is through computerized listservs—electronic discussion groups for people with common interests—that include participants around the United States.

- *Resource assessment.* A preliminary review of available resources (staff time, currently active programs, facilities, money, institutional support) contributes to the needs assessment. Program planners should also get a sense of what other services are currently available in the library and elsewhere on campus in order to identify what else may need to be done or what modifications may be appropriately introduced.

- *National picture.* A needs assessment may also include some consideration of nationwide conditions regarding, for example, minority college retention. This will help place the local scene in a broader context and give some idea of the scope of issues.

Methodology

Needs assessment uses the same methods as any research process. Basic methods are (1) a survey of the general population; (2) a survey of the target population; (3) interviews with other service providers or key members of the target population; (4) a review of "social indicators" (for example, minority student graduation rates from the institution); and (5) a review of administrative and other documents or records (Rothman and Gant, 37).

A survey can help to track down "consumer" views. Representation on a survey should be across the board. The easiest way to administer a survey is to pass out questionnaires to students who are in the library. Many students will be left out that way, perhaps even a large segment of the minority population. Questionnaires should be distributed elsewhere—the student union, residence halls, the school bookstore—or mailed to all constituents in order to capture a wider respondent base. Questionnaires should also have some open-ended questions to allow respondents to clarify their answers.

Examples of user surveys abound in the literature (see, for example, University of Texas; Lubans; Lawton). A library needs assessment survey at Gullaudet University is an example of a survey geared toward needs assessment. All students, staff, and faculty members were asked to respond to a survey specifically designed for their group. Each survey included a list of possible library instruction services and asked respondents to rate each according to interest and likelihood of use. There was also an open-ended section for comments or suggestions. The library also offered to send a summary of results to any respondents.

A survey is a good way to obtain a large number of responses. Interviews or focus groups (small group interviews) give respondents a chance to elaborate on their responses and to interact with the researcher. When used with a survey, interviews help to round out the needs assessment.

A review of documents and "indicators" adds additional perspectives to the needs assessment. Together these methods should illustrate the current state of library service and campus attitudes toward them, some idea of what the community perceives to be an "ideal" or at least an improved state, and suggestions for what programs will move library service from its current situation toward the ideal.

SETTING GOALS AND OBJECTIVES

The critical question on which everything else hangs is, What does the library hope to accomplish in creating this new program? There is much in the library literature about the necessity of formalizing goals and objectives, but they are still easy to overlook in the press of starting something new, particularly if there is an administrative or campus-wide push to put new initiatives into place quickly. Program planners often rush to respond to campus trends and external, perhaps political, pressures to "do something" to resolve a perceived problem such as low minority retention rates.

Setting goals and objectives at the outset, however, will help avoid some problems later. It will certainly ease the process of setting up a new activity. Here are several important reasons to set goals early:

- Goals and objectives help to focus the program and keep it realistic. By outlining exactly what you hope to achieve and what direction the program will take, specific goals keep activities manageable.
- In becoming more focused, the program planner can be more effective because it has been made clear exactly what is expected of the program. The

planner or coordinator knows what should receive the most attention and effort and what can slide.

- Clear objectives help others to understand the program. This includes both library administrators (or others who may also provide program support) as well as staff and even participants, if the objectives are shared with them. The goals and objectives can help to justify the program and also show that planners have given the program some thought. Written goals and objectives make it evident that the program is well-grounded.

- Writing objectives can help the program coordinator to be learner-focused. Many librarians think about instruction or patron contact in terms of what information they want to pass on to the students. Goals and objectives written from the point of view of the library user, that is, in terms of what the library user should be able to do after instruction is completed, will keep attention where it should be: on the student and the student's developing skills.

- Last and certainly not least, goals and objectives help librarians determine if the program actually arrived at its destination. When it comes time to evaluate, the objectives act as standards against which the evaluator can measure the program's achievements.

The labels used vary from one writer to the next, but goals and objectives are often presented in three levels: goals or general objectives, terminal objectives, and enabling or performance objectives. Goals or general objectives are defined as the overall intent or purpose of a program, the general statement about what the library wishes to achieve. A sample goal might be the following: "To improve the library use skills of at-risk students in order to assist them in becoming better students and help them to complete their college education."

Terminal and enabling objectives identify specific elements of the overarching goal. Terminal objectives break the goals down into meaningful units (Roberts and Blandy, 30), as in the following examples, which expand on the above goal:

- Students are aware of resources and support available to them in the library.
- Students are able to use basic finding tools, such as the catalog, in conducting their research.
- Students feel positive about using the library and are comfortable in the library.
- Students recognize peer counselors as sources of assistance.

Enabling or performance objectives are the most specific. Enabling objectives define specific knowledge, behaviors, or skills to be achieved

Figure 6.1
Structuring Performance Objectives

(Roberts and Blandy, 30). They specify exactly how you will determine that the goals have been reached. One way to structure performance objectives, described by Janet Freedman and Harold Bantly, is summarized in Figure 6.1.

The task is the skill or behavior the student is to display; the condition is how the task is carried out; and the standard is usually a measurable factor. So, for example, a performance objective might read: Using the online catalog, the student can locate three books relevant to a research project in ten minutes.

The condition is "using the online catalog," and the standard is "three books in ten minutes." The task is to locate books. The most useful objectives are that specific. You know exactly what the target is; at evaluation time, it is easy to determine if the target was hit. Here are some other examples of somewhat less specific but nevertheless acceptable objectives:

- The student asks for assistance from a peer counselor (or other staff member) when faced with a question s/he cannot answer.
- Given a research problem, the student can name special library services available to provide support (e.g., term paper assistance program, peer counseling, and database searching).
- The student can describe the basic services of the peer counseling program.

The task outlined in the objectives must be realistic and learnable. They should also reflect the library's resources not only in terms of materials, but also in terms of the staff time, money, facilities, and so forth available to provide assistance to students (Roberts and Blandy, 31). The best objectives are worthless if the library does not have the staff, the space, or the financial support to implement them.

The language of objectives is very concrete. They use action verbs such as identify, name, define, select, list, write, or describe, instead of verbs such as understand, appreciate, or know. They describe observable and measurable behaviors to be demonstrated by the learner.

Terminal and performance or enabling objectives may be written for peer counselors or other program staff members as well:

- Terminal objective: At the beginning of the fall semester, the program coordinator will hire and train five students to act as peer counselors.
- Enabling objectives: Each peer counselor will complete the training course within one month after being hired. Each peer counselor will attend five dormitory teaching sessions in the fall term and three in the winter term.

Objectives can be difficult to write. Many people are not accustomed to breaking ideas down into small, concrete segments. There is no cut and dried method for producing objectives. One method is to work in a small group, scribbling ideas on a chalkboard and making changes on the spot as the group brainstorms (Breivik, 65). Brainstorm and write down everything that might be desirable, even those that are merely pipe dreams. You can winnow out what is truly possible later. Another approach is to review the statement of goals and objectives for similar programs or model program statements and modify what has already been prepared by others. Goals and objectives written for bibliographic instruction programs can lend themselves very well to a peer counseling program, and there are numerous examples of model statements. Goals and objectives for reference are another useful source.

A typical pattern is to start by writing the goals, then working down to the specific enabling objectives. It is not unreasonable, however, to take the opposite approach, writing the most specific elements, clustering them, then writing the terminal objectives based on what has been written and, finally, the goals (Clark and Jones, 55). Either approach can result in usable and meaningful goals and objectives.

SETTING REALISTIC GOALS

When determining the final goals and objectives, it is important to be realistic. Now is the time to mesh needs with resources. Campus needs may be well beyond what the library can handle. Assessing needs in relation to resources will help identify to what degree the library can meet those needs. Consider the following factors when assessing the practicality of proposed goals and objectives:

Staff. What does the current staff bring to the program, and what can they reasonably accomplish? Consider not only staff size, but their skills and experience. Another staff issue is departmental commitments. If the staff is already stretched thin, they may be able to contribute little to new programming. Program planners should also determine the staff's attitude toward the proposed plan. Some might view it as a exciting opportunity, while others might resent any new program as a burden. Time must be taken to win staff commitment to a new program or to determine ways to limit the burden on those who are not prepared to take on additional responsibilities, otherwise the new program may not get off the ground.

Supervisor. If one person will be handling program responsibilities, how will his or her current tasks be handled? Can work be distributed differently? What clerical, paraprofessional, or professional support will be available to the coordinator?

Money. Financial support is possibly the biggest area of concern. What kind of budget is likely to be available? Is there a possibility of outside funding, or does the program go forward on the current budget?

Politics. What is the current political atmosphere on campus? How well is your program going to be received? Will it be perceived as taking money away from other areas, or will it be considered an enhancement to the academic environment? Will members of your target group be sensitive to possible implications that they require special help?

Administration. What kind of administrative support is forthcoming? Even if no financial support is available, administration both within and outside of the library will be instrumental in moving the program forward—or stopping it in its tracks. Will other big initiatives or problems—for example, a statewide mandated budget cut—distract from efforts to implement a special program?

Collection. What kind of collection support is there? Does the collection adequately support the initiative? If a successful program will mean more students using the collection, are there enough materials? Do the materials reflect interests of potential new user groups?

Not all of these questions can be answered readily. Some of the answers may be based only on the impressions of planners or perhaps some supportive colleagues. Though the answers may not be definitive, they are, nevertheless, valuable.

PROGRAM DEVELOPMENT

Once the program is in place it will still need to respond to changing user needs. Evaluation (discussed in Chapter 9) will be critical in helping the program to remain current and meaningful to a constantly new student population. A number of factors may shift over time. For example, in some places librarians are seeing students who are increasingly computer-literate. Fewer and fewer students need basic instruction in computer use.

Those who need assistance should not get lost in the crowd, but those who do not need help will find a program that concentrates solely on the basics of no use. Talking with students will give some guidance regarding the level of their information skills and what new skills they need or want to develop. If online catalogs are familiar territory, boolean operators may still be a mystery. If *Social Sciences Index* does not pose a challenge, *Psychological Abstracts* or PsycInfo on CD-ROM might spark some interest. As students become more sophisticated as a group, so must services.

On the other hand, if the university or college is actively recruiting at-risk students, the library may in fact begin to see students with weaker library skills. Again, a shift in service or program emphasis can accommodate a new user base.

Significant changes on campus or in the library can be excellent springboards for new programs or new program activities. The implementation of an online catalog or other automation such as CD-ROMs, or a new academic program such as Hispanic Studies, presents opportunities for making the most of a peer counseling service. Students wanting to know about the new online catalog, for example, might be directed to the desk of the new catalog experts, trained peer counselors, for immediate instruction. The counselors may also take their skills out into the campus community, offering sessions on the catalog in the dormitories or fraternity and sorority houses, or for student groups. Not only is this the initiation of expanded service, it is also a chance to increase program visibility.

New forms of communication present another opportunity for the library to exploit. Many campuses have their own newspapers, but other publications also spring up from time to time, and these can be approached as a means to reach new audiences through advertising. Increasingly widespread, too, are online conferences or electronic mailboxes. The program coordinator might consider training library peer counselors to teach the use of electronic communication to other students. In addition, online conferences and other electronic communication systems are useful modes of publicity. And certainly the counselors would benefit greatly from using these mechanisms, perhaps setting up a peer counselor electronic mailbox to keep in touch with program users.

To keep up with changing campus trends, maintain contact with the network of other campus service providers and with appropriate faculty and students. Meet with them informally over coffee or in their offices and attend open houses or other departmental functions whenever possible. In the library these faculty, student, and staff contacts are on the librarian's turf. Getting out of the library and seeing students and faculty in settings more familiar to them might be revealing. Of course, it is also helpful to keep up with student publications, new information from appropriate offices such as Minority Affairs or Admissions, and other sources of campus information.

Periodically revisit the early steps of the original planning process: the needs assessment, community analysis, and goals and objectives. Both needs assessment and community analysis may, in fact, need to be redone from time to time. Program coordinators should periodically determine if there have been pertinent changes in the student population which could be addressed by new program services. Some changes may or may not be obvious to the library staff member on the desk. As the cost of higher education skyrockets, institutions may see a rise in the number of commuters or part-time students, for example. A little systematic information gathering may be needed to get the new picture in focus.

Changes in resources may stimulate program changes: adding or eliminating a professional position, a new staff member with new skills and interests, the acquisition of a departmental video cassette recorder, an increase in the student employee budget—any of a number of changes can offer ideas and opportunities for new program initiatives.

Program evaluation will help program organizers to assess the appropriateness of the goals and objectives. In addition to this formal review, the goals and objectives can be looked at each time a program status report is written and informally assessed by library staff or the program coordinator. If the initial goals were broadly written, there will be flexibility to change the objectives. At some point perhaps even more extensive modifications will become necessary.

As program changes are made, the goals and objectives should be kept up to date and shared with library administrators and program sponsors. This helps them to stay in the know if anyone should contact them directly about library activities. It may trigger thoughts and suggestions on their part as well. It also demonstrates that the program is not simply haphazardly put together, but is a legitimate and purposeful activity subject to sound planning processes.

Marketing, often an unpopular concept in libraries, is nevertheless part of what we do when developing and publicizing library services and programs. We read our audience and try to determine what they want by consulting them, by consulting ourselves, and by consulting other "experts." As their tastes, interests, and needs change, we change, and we hope we are developing our product into something continuously appealing to our audience. Some of our approaches are formal—surveys, focus groups, interviews—and others are informal—casual conversations, suggestion boxes, observation. We are constantly gathering data even when we are not actively aware of it. All of this goes into the mix and, we hope, eventually comes out as a viable and beneficial, even "profitable," service to students, one with real impact on their educational experience.

REFERENCES

Breivik, Patricia. *Planning the Library Program.* Chicago: American Library Association, 1982.

Clark, Alice, and Kay F. Jones. "Writing Objectives: Methodology and Examples." In *Teaching Librarians to Teach.* Metuchen, N.J.: Scarecrow, 1986.

Freedman, Janet, and Harold Bantly. *Information Searching: A Handbook for Creating and Designing Instruction.* Metuchen, N.J.: Scarecrow, 1982.

Hobbs, Daryl. "Strategy for Needs Assessment." In *Needs Assessment: Theory and Methods.* Edited by Donald E. Johnson et al. Ames: Iowa State University Press, 1987.

Kirk, Thomas. "Problems in Library Instruction in Four-Year Colleges." In *Educating the Library User.* Edited by John Lubans, Jr. New York: Bowker, 1974.

Lawton, Bethany. "Library Instruction Needs Assessment: Designing Survey Instruments." *Research Strategies* 7, no. 3 (Summer 1989), 119–128.

Lubans, John, Jr. "Evaluating Library-User Education Programs." In *Educating the Library User.* Edited by John Lubans, Jr. New York: Bowker, 1977.

Newhouse, Robert. "A Library Essential: Needs Assessment." *Library Reviews* 39, no. 2 (1990), 33–36.

Renford, Beverly, and Linnea Hendrickson. *Bibliographic Instruction: A Handbook.* New York: Neal-Schuman, 1980.

Rice, James, Jr. *Teaching Library Use.* Westport, Conn.: Greenwood Press, 1981.

Roberts, Anne F., and Susan G. Blandy. *Library Instruction for Librarians.* Englewood, Colo.: Libraries Unlimited, 1989.

Rothman, Jack, and Larry Gant. "Approaches and Models of Community Intervention." In *Needs Assessment: Theory and Methods.* Edited by Donald E. Johnson et al. Ames: Iowa State University Press, 1987.

University of Texas at Austin. General Libraries. *Comprehensive Program of User Education for the General Libraries.* Austin: University of Texas at Austin, General Libraries, 1977.

7

Building a Campus Network

On large university campuses, making any program visible is a challenging task. Advertising and marketing are invaluable means to achieve recognition of a program. However, personal contact with other student services personnel and teaching faculty is often the best way for a library program to receive valuable referrals. The referrals that the library receives from colleagues across campus are often the best method of getting timid or apprehensive students to begin using the program's services. All library staff have a responsibility to promote the services of the program whenever appropriate.

ESTABLISHING THE CAMPUS NETWORK

Establishing a network of contact people around campus is vital to your program for several reasons:

- Keeping your services relevant. Campus contacts will alert you to what is going on around campus, which will help keep your services relevant to your students.
- Referrals. Since you cannot be at all places on campus at once, your campus contacts will refer students to you if they know you can help.
- Support. Contacts will muster support across campus for your programs if your services are viewed as tying in to what they do.
- Publicity. Assistance in passing the word along about your services is always needed on large campuses.

Setting up a strong campus network takes a person who loves people, is not shy about getting together with strangers, is comfortable selling the program over and over again, and is willing to risk rejection once in a while. It also takes someone who views every campus meeting or event as a possible opportunity to sell the program or meet a new contact. Good program promoters never stop selling their goods and services!

Identifying Appropriate Units and Personnel

Begin by identifying other units and colleagues that share some of your overall goals. Fostering academic achievement, empowering students, and developing critical thinking skills are goals shared by many other student services units and personnel, teaching faculty, and campus administrators. Once you have identified the units on campus to target, compile a list of contacts. There are several ways to develop this list:

1. *Use the campus directory.* Every campus has some sort of directory listing all units, departments, and offices. Take time to go through the directory thoroughly to identify other units, and the people within those units, that may be helpful to or supportive of your program's goals. The task may seem tedious, but it is essential. You will probably discover units and positions that you had no idea existed before. This only reinforces the need to be visible on campus.

2. *Ask students for their contacts.* If there are students already working at the library, or students who have a close relationship with librarians on staff, use their knowledge of the campus to add names to your list of contacts. Students have a keen sense of who on campus is really interested in their success and the contacts they provide can be valuable.

3. *Begin with obvious units and get their input.* Begin with units such as Minority Student Services or Academic Counseling. Once you have established a relationship with these people, ask their advice on how to proceed. Ask them whom they partner with on campus. They will have suggestions about who may be willing to help publicize your program, or who will be valuable in sending you referrals.

Most campuses will have offices or units similar to the following:

- Housing Office. The staff that work directly with new students within the residence halls provide a valuable link to new students. They include resident assistants, building directors, minority peer advisors, etc.

- Office of Minority Affairs. Every campus has some office where special services for students of color are coordinated.

- Athletic Department Counseling Office. This has direct ties to the student athletes and assists them with academic work.

- Student Affairs Office. Staff will know the student groups and their leaders.

- Academic Affairs Office. Counselors here will know which students need extra help with academics. Visibility with this office is very important.

- American Culture departments and African, Latin American, and Asian Studies departments. Students of color often take classes in these disciplines. Strong ties with teaching faculty in these and other departments are important.

- Summer Bridge Program Offices. Many universities offer summer enhancement programs for specially admitted students. Setting up a strong relationship with these offices is very important because these students need your help.

- Office of Orientation. Most orientation offices send incoming students packets of information and have some of the first contacts with new students. Make sure they know about your program.

How to Strengthen Contacts

Now that you have developed a list of contacts, what do you do with it? There are several ways to keep in touch regularly with your contacts.

1. *Create a comprehensive mailing list.* Creating a mailing list is a fast, easy way to keep in touch with a maximum number of strategic people throughout campus. Using the campus directory, page through the listings of units to find who might be interested in receiving information about your program. If you have secretarial or clerical support, you can simply highlight the units and people you wish to include. The secretary or student can then go through the directory and type up a master mailing label list and run off several copies of mailing labels for you. Each summer the list should be updated.

- Get on other units' mailing lists too. It helps to keep an eye on what is going on with related units on campus so that you can offer your support and services to them. Ask other units if they keep a mailing list, if they distribute a newsletter, or if they publish any literature of their own. This is an excellent way to keep up on campus events and to tie in your services to other units' priorities.

- Seek out lists of minority faculty and staff personnel. Some campuses have comprehensive lists of minority faculty and staff. These lists can assist you in reaching out to key persons who may have contact with large numbers of students of color. They can be excellent advocates for your program and services to the students who need you most.

2. *Campus visitations.* Getting out of the office and meeting people on their own turf is often a good idea. People feel comfortable in their own environments, and will appreciate your taking the time and interest to come to see them. Visiting various units takes lots more time than sending out materials in a mass mailing, but often the time taken pays for itself many times over in the returns you will see in the end. The personal contact is what your colleagues across campus will remember.

Because campus visits are so time-consuming, it may be best before you begin to set priorities to determine which units or people will be most important in passing along the word about your services. A student services unit that has contact with hundreds of students each month may be your best contact, or you may wish to concentrate on a smaller unit that specializes in a specific student population. For example, the Native American support group leader may not bring in large numbers of students, but the contact that individual has with his or her constituency is very influential, and therefore may pay off better in the end.

Deciding with whom, where, and when to meet can be difficult. Some standard ways to arrange these meetings include:

- Lunch meetings. Luncheon arrangements are almost always a good way to make strong connections with campus individuals or groups. Perhaps one day a week could be set aside for lunch with a rotating group or individuals. The atmosphere lunch meetings is often more personal and comfortable than the office setting. Again, people will remember you on a personal level as well as the message you bring professionally.

- Campus functions. Your colleagues in the library may wonder why you attend so many campus functions, but this is often the very best time to meet possible contacts throughout the campus. Watch the campus newspaper or faculty/staff newsletter for notices of events for special campus groups or units.

- Departmental meetings. Asking for a few minutes on the agenda of a meeting within a targeted department is a great way to reach a number of individuals at once. The personal contact is made, and you can supplement this contact with additional mailings.

- Student organization meetings. Most student organizations meet monthly, or at least have a regular meeting schedule. Determine when these organizations meet by contacting the student affairs office to get the names of student leaders for each target organization. By contacting these students personally, or assigning one of your peer students to each group, you will build a natural bridge between those students and your services.

- Individual meetings with unit heads. If a meeting with a department or unit does not fit into your schedule or theirs, meeting with the unit head is often the next best thing. Impress on this individual the importance of passing along the information to his or her colleagues. Following up with periodic mailings is an effective way to keep up these important contacts.

- Meetings with large campus groups. For example, athletic teams are one type of large campus group that would be useful to target. Having strong contacts with athletic advisors is important. Most campuses with strong athletic departments employ a handful of academic advisors specifically for student athletes. They meet individually with the students and with the teams as a whole. If you can present your services at a team meeting, or at least meet with the advisors or coaches to let them know you support their academic goals for student athletes, you will begin a strong relationship which is potentially very beneficial for the students.

- Meetings with other groups. Numerous groups form on campus that may be potential links in your network. The trick is finding them and contacting the leader. Watch the campus papers and take time to read flyers, notices, and so on, to see what groups are sponsoring activities. At the University of Michigan, the campus Greeks sponsor an alcohol awareness week each fall. The Undergraduate Library partners with this event by providing information and bibliographies on the topic prepared by peer counseling students and librarians. Partnerships like this are very valuable in building and sustaining a strong campus network.

3. *Determine which faculty members will be teaching minority-relevant courses.* Keep close tabs on the schedule of classes each semester. This will provide you with names of professors who are teaching courses of special interest to your target audience. Send your materials to these professors, use electronic mail to keep in touch, and try to drop in on them at the beginning of each semester to see if they know of any students who may need your services.

4. *Determine in which departments minority students are concentrating.* On many campuses it is possible to contact the registrar's office to determine which departments your target students are majoring in. Those are the departments to emphasize in your visitations and other means of contact.

5. *Put on your own functions and invite your campus network.* Holding an open house in the library is an ideal way to get people into the facilities in an informal and nonthreatening manner. If possible, serve refreshments. Send out invitations to all campus network people via your comprehensive mailing list, and send out invitations to all your target students as well. A personal computer can be used to design the invitations, and printing them on card stock is easy and inexpensive (see Figure 7.1). Send them through

Figure 7.1
Sample Invitation

COME CELEBRATE WITH US!

The staff at the Undergraduate Library and the
Comprehensive Studies Program requests your presence.
In order to celebrate the successful completion
of the 1st college year by the Bridge students,
a reception will be held in the Lobby of the UGL on
FRIDAY, APRIL 24th
from 3:30 – 5:00 pm.

Refreshments will be served.

campus mail to further cut expense. Have plenty of peer counselors on hand for this event, along with a few librarians. Have available demonstrations of your online catalog, literature on the program services, and a variety of your most useful and attractive handouts.

6. *Offer your services to them.* Developing and strengthening the campus network is not a one-way street. Your contacts must feel that they are getting something from the relationship as well. If they feel their students are benefiting from your services, that is enough to get referrals, but getting something extra, such as tutorials on the online catalog for themselves and their staff, creates a special link between the library and their units.

HOW TO KEEP THE CAMPUS NETWORK STRONG AND VITAL

On larger campuses in particular, it is essential to keep in regular contact with network members. If contact is sporadic and infrequent, network members will not automatically think of referring students to the library.

1. *Electronic mail/conferences.* Many larger campuses now have resources available for staff, students, and faculty to electronically message one another. Many campuses with these facilities also have set up electronic conferences where anyone can sign in and discuss a particular issue. The University of Michigan has several conferences which many target students sign onto on a regular basis. Using these

electronic resources can be a tremendous time-saving way to keep in close and regular contact with faculty, staff, and students in your network.

Usually the campus technology division will provide all staff with electronic "accounts." Each month, or on a regular basis, you are allotted funds which you can use to send messages to people on your campus and campuses across the country. Your campus computing center or technology division can teach you how to use these systems and can assist you with signing up for an account.

2. *Regular planned meetings*. Develop a core group of supporters from across campus based on who responds positively to your services. Meet regularly with these individuals in an informal setting. Meeting for lunch once a month allows you to keep track of what their units are doing and how their jobs are going, and allows you to let them know how your program is progressing.

3. *Symbiotic relationship*. Offer your services; use theirs.

4. *Regular mailings*. Regular mailings using your comprehensive mailing list will accomplish what you and your colleagues cannot do in person—reach a large number of people on a regular basis. Sending them news of special programs and new library services alerts them to useful library facts while reminding them of your program and the need for referrals. Some useful publications include newsletters; handouts explaining new electronic tools, library policies and procedures, and so on; bibliographies on current topics; and items that promote the program, for example, pens and pencils, stadium cups, or program brochures.

5. *Ask them to hand out your program/service brochure in their offices*. Most student services units on campus will be pleased to hand out your brochures if they are aware of the importance of your services and if the brochures are well written and attractive. You could ask unit heads to display twenty-five copies of your brochure, then send them out with a note thanking them for their interest in your program. Offer to reciprocate the service by posting their brochures or flyers in the library.

6. *Visibility through any means possible!* It will take several semesters of trying combinations of all the above methods of building your network before you find the mix that best fits your contacts and your style. Visibility is one of the most important factors in making your peer program reach its goal of connecting the students with the library's services.

REFERENCES

Lewis, Jerry J. "The Black Freshman Network." *College & University* 61, no. 2 (Winter 1986), 135–40.

Noel, L. "College Retention—A Campus-Wide Responsibility." *Journal of the National Association of College Admissions Counselors* 21 (1976), 33–36.
Simmons, R., and C. Maxwell-Simmons. *Principles of Success in Programs for Minority Students.* Hoboken, N.J.: Stevens Institute of Technology, 1978.

8

Marketing and Public Relations

Marketing, broadly defined, includes all the functions necessary to develop and "sell" library services to end users. This includes developing relevant services, client research, and advertising. Because so many programs and services vie for attention these days on campuses of any size, it is imperative to publicize your program as much as time and money allow. Usually, once students know about your services and understand why they are important to their success, they will use them repeatedly. The challenge for librarians is to make users aware of the services available. On large campuses publicity and exposure present a special challenge because there are many campus units promoting their own agendas, and thus more programs with which to compete for students' attention. While exposure must be ongoing and thorough, publicity does not have to cost an arm and a leg; a few brochures, flyers, posters, newsletters, and network contacts will go a long way if they are designed and planned well. Publicity for the program should combine both direct and indirect marketing methods in order to ensure that the greatest number of target students are reached.

DIRECT AND INDIRECT MARKETING METHODS

Use a combination of direct and indirect marketing methods to reach the greatest number of target students. "Direct marketing efforts are calculated to elicit a direct response on the part of potential customers." In this case, direct marketing would be aimed at the end user (Ostrow, 74).

Direct methods, those aimed directly at the end users, could include mailing out newsletters, brochures, and program announcements; handing out flyers to students around campus; announcements in bibliographic instruction (B.I.) classes; and telling students at the reference desk or other settings about the services. Indirect marketing is meant to stimulate future use of services by end users (Ostrow, 117). Indirect methods of marketing include efforts to publicize the program through intermediaries such as teaching faculty, student counselors, admissions staff, student services representatives, residence hall staff, and so on.

Marketing Research

In order to choose an appropriate mix of direct and indirect marketing methods it is essential to do the following:

1. *Know who your target audience is.* By formulating a special service program, you have already determined that a specific group of students needs your services. While setting up your program objectives and goals, learn all you can about your target populations. If you have not done so already, this is the time to find out as much about these students as possible. For instance, find out from the registrar's office the percentage of students of color on campus. You may want to know in what areas of study students of color on your campus are concentrating. What is the retention rate for your target audience? These pieces of information can be used to tailor your publicity (as well as your program goals and objectives) to your target audience. While gathering valuable information to aid your program development, you will also be able to design advertisements and publicity brochures that will speak to these users' needs. The idea is to have your advertisements hit home with the students who read them.

2. *Conduct focus groups.* If you can procure a mailing list for your target students from the registrar's office, it is valuable to conduct a few focus group sessions to determine firsthand what services students want and need. Armed with this information, take the opportunity to ask their opinion on how effective different advertising campaigns would be. Also ask them about advertising methods: which methods leave a lasting impression, and which are forgotten soon after exposure?

3. *Develop interesting and relevant services or products.* Once you have determined that your services are needed, you must prove it to your target group(s). Many students, when confronted with the opportunity to use the library and its services, are not stimulated and excited. The challenge here is to make your services sound interesting and intriguing and to make the students feel welcome to inquire about and use them. Emphasizing that

peer assistants are undergraduate students like themselves should make users feel more willing to inquire about the services offered. If you stress self-empowerment through information literacy, users may be motivated to check out what the library has to offer. Playing up the exciting aspect of learning to access computerized information may encourage users to learn a relevant skill. Push any other aspects of your services that may turn their heads or grab their attention.

Emphasize how your services will improve their performance and ultimately save them time. If the benefits to your target students are not understood quickly and easily in an advertisement or a meeting, they will tune you out before you ever have a chance. Improved performance and time-saving skills are concrete reasons for them to remember your program.

4. *Big budget versus small budget advertising.* There are plenty of ways you can promote your program even if you do not have a big advertising budget. When your budget is less than generous, quality rather than quantity is the key to a successful advertising campaign. Design a few key pieces that will catch people's attention and that you will be able to use in more than one method of advertising.

For instance, if you design a poster to display in residence and lecture halls, you can include the same design elements in a small flyer (see Appendix Three) that can be produced less expensively in larger quantities. Or you could mail that same flyer directly to your target students and to your colleagues and acquaintances across campus.

5. *Work with professional graphics people if the budget will allow.* Most institutions with a professional design or commercial art curriculum will offer campus units some sort of design shop assistance. Art or design students may be willing to work at a much reduced fee to design some advertising pieces which they can then put in their portfolio. Sometimes a project like this can be done for academic credit rather than pay. Art students may need a bit of extra time because of their inexperience, but their sense of design and style (they are closer to the target audience than many experienced commercial artists) is sure to be advantageous.

If your budget is a bit more generous, look into the possibility of using your campus graphics department or an outside contractor. Professional graphic artists' design sense and knowledge of what will get a person's attention are invaluable. They can also help you to use one main design in more than one way. If your budget allows, use the work of professional photographers and artists to draw attention to your ads. Once again, many campuses have a publications or news department that can be a source of less expensive photography or original artwork.

WHERE TO ADVERTISE

Once you have developed some interesting advertisements, you will have to consider many different venues for promoting your program. Keep it in the forefront of people's minds, through diligent use of communication and publicity. On a large campus with a multitude of activities and organizations, people need frequent reminders of your services and programs.

Direct Methods of Advertising

Direct advertising methods include those that address the target audience without an intermediary. Examples include direct mailings, one-on-one talking, one-on-many lectures, and so on. To assist in keeping up regular direct contact with your targeted students:

1. *Create a comprehensive mailing list.* You must determine to whom you will be directly marketing your program. This means first creating a comprehensive mailing list of all targeted students on campus. Work with the campus registrar's office and appropriate administrators. Most universities have computerized records, allowing you to specify how you want your list sorted. For example, if you need a list of all undergraduate students of color who live in campus residence halls, this can be easily accomplished.

2. *Advertise programs during Bibliographic Instruction classes and tours.* During bibliographic instruction classes you have a captive audience, so to speak. Use a small portion of the time while conducting a class tour to alert students to your special services. Emphasize the benefits of the services you offer and welcome them to ask for help at any time. To remind students of the services after the class or tour is finished, give them a brochure or flyer to take with them.

3. *Advertise programs when you attend student functions on campus.* An important duty of any coordinator of a special service or program is to attend various functions, meetings, and gatherings across campus. When attending a special showing of a film or a demonstration of a dance as part of an ethnic heritage celebration, remember that this is a student function. You are on their turf, and you have an opportunity to promote your services to students individually or as a group. You may wish to ask student leaders who organize educational programs to include you formally in a program agenda, or you may wish to attend informally. Either way, students will know you care when you take time to attend their functions and meetings and to inform them about your services.

4. *Promote programs at the reference desk.* Use the time at the reference desk to let students know about your special services. If a student is anxious about using the online catalog or needs a bit more help than you can provide on the spot, make an appointment for the student with a peer assistant right then and there.

5. *Hold an open house.* Using the space within the library for a fun and informal get-together for students will create a positive association toward the library early on and encourage students to return. If you have a separate room in which functions can be held and refreshments served, invite students in to see firsthand what you have to offer. Give out freebies such as tee shirts, pencils, pens, and posters, that will remind them of the library and its services. Make announcements on the public address system before and during the event to alert students who may be unaware of it. Use table tents, campus newspaper ads, flyers, and so on, to publicize the event beforehand.

6. *Advertise in student publications.* Every campus has a variety of student publications that will be happy to have you advertise for a fee. Some may even be aimed at a specific segment of the student population, such as students of color. Contact the campus news and information service department or the student publications office for a list of publications.

- Daily paper. Most campuses have a student newspaper, usually written and produced by students. Publication frequency varies, but most are published at least once a week. This is a very good way to reach students. However, it can be expensive to place a sizable display ad. A less costly option is to place a classified ad in the student services section describing your services. A disadvantage is that classified ads are less eye-catching for the casual reader.

- Minority student publications. Many black sororities and fraternities publish yearbooks, though usually at the end of the year, in which advertisements can be placed. This is a good way to reach a target audience at a very reasonable cost. On some campuses student organizations publish newsletters or papers targeted at specific groups, such as minority, international, or disabled students. Contact the appropriate student service department to determine which organizations produce these publications.

7. *Orientation for new students.* Some campuses have orientation for all new students. Some also have special orientation and welcoming sessions for students of color. Try to be included in these events. They are often jam-packed already, so you may have to convince the orientation planners that new students need to know about your program.

Indirect Methods of Advertising

Indirect methods of advertising services use intermediaries in order to reach end users. It is necessary to have a strong network of library advocates across campus in order for indirect methods to work.

1. *Nonstudent campus publications.* Many other units and departments on campus send out newsletters to students, staff, and faculty. This is a good vehicle for letting the entire campus community know about your services.

- Call or send a memorandum to all related student-oriented units on campus to determine which units publish newsletters. Ask to be put on their mailing list and put them on your mailing list as well.

- It is a good idea to ask for some space in these publications to increase awareness of your program. Usually newsletter editors from other units are only too happy to have something new to write about in their publications.

2. *Letters and networking.* Several times a year, remind colleagues and acquaintances who have access to your target users of your services and programs. This can be accomplished by simply giving them a quick call and asking if they know of any students who might benefit from your services. Another way of reminding your colleagues is to send out a mass mailing of a letter stating the objectives, goals, and services of your program. Enclosing a publication such as a bibliography on a particular ethnic group or a copy of your newsletter is also a nice way to further emphasize your program's scope. Mailings such as this are relatively quick and easy once you have a master mailing list. You can enlist your students' help with stuffing envelopes and even with writing the letter. Perhaps an illustration of a "success story" would urge your colleagues to refer other students to you as well.

Perhaps the best way to use your network people is by a combination of the phone call and mass mailing along with more formal meetings where you can talk with a group of colleagues all at once. This can be as time-intensive as you wish to make it. For example, rather than meeting with admissions counselors individually, it makes sense to meet with them all at one time at a prearranged staff meeting. The same is true of residence hall staff, academic advisors, and so on. Most departments have staff meeting times and would allow you to meet with them for at least part of a normal session.

To assist in keeping up contacts with colleagues on a regular basis, develop a comprehensive mailing list of units, people, and departments that support student services. Using a campus directory, browse through the listing of departments and people within those units (and their titles) to develop a comprehensive list of names and addresses. You will use this list many times, so develop it with much time and care. Once the list is made, you can transfer the names and addresses to mailing labels that can be run off on a photocopier whenever you need to do a mailing. Students can assist with keeping the list current by crossing off old names if something is returned, or by reviewing the campus directory each summer.

Within your valuable network of campus contacts lie many years of experience in promoting their own programs and agendas. Most colleagues are only too happy to share their knowledge about successful ways of reaching students and other target populations. Ask your colleagues for ideas on reaching your target populations. Bounce new ideas for publicity off them to get their reaction. Always remember that this type of information sharing is a two-way street, and be willing to share your experience as well.

3. *Newsletters*. Two functions are served by producing your own publications: you are passing along valuable information about the library and its resources, and you are producing a valuable piece of advertising for your services.

It is advisable to publish a newsletter at least twice during the academic year. The first issue should be mailed or otherwise distributed during the first several weeks of the fall semester. The idea is to "get them while they're young" and impress upon them the importance of developing good library skills early on. It is always best to distribute the newsletters to students before they get too bogged down with school work, while they have time to learn about the online catalog or how to use indexes or Library of Congress call numbers. The second issue should be distributed at the beginning of the winter semester to reinforce their knowledge of your program and services. This is also the time to advertise for students for the following school year.

Mail the newsletters to as many of your target students as possible and have them available to pick-up within the library and at various student service units on campus. When the student mailing is finished, send them to colleagues and network people.

4. *Flyers*. An inexpensive method of alerting students to your services is to post flyers around campus. This should be done on a regular basis, perhaps once a month. The flyers should be cleanly designed so that they won't look like student ads for roommates, parties, and other events. Check campus regulations on posting flyers. Some of the most common locations include residence halls, lecture halls, campus bulletin boards and kiosks,

all the libraries on campus, campus computing centers, student support service units, campus housing office, minority student services, student counseling office, academic advising, and so on. Check your campus directory for listings of units relevant to your program.

5. *Bus signs.* If your campus runs a bus service for commuters, a cross-campus shuttle, or a similar service, chances are that advertising space can be rented for any period of time you wish on the interior or exterior of the buses. It is usually a bargain, but you may be required to provide the advertisements yourself. Again, if you have a poster or flyer that can be adapted to the space constraints of a bus sign, this is an effective way to promote the program.

6. *Displays and bulletin boards.* Most libraries put together rotating displays that are exhibited anywhere from a week to several months. If your library has display space in a prominent area, use it to convey information about your program. Use photographs of your peer advisors or use some of your program publications, brochures, and flyers. Many other student gathering places, such as the student union, student activities buildings, or campus computing centers, may also have display space to rent or loan to you for a nice-looking exhibit.

7. *Information fairs.* At the beginning of each academic year, information fairs are usually sponsored by the housing departments, graduate school's new teaching assistants, and other groups. The library may not be invited automatically. To get into the action, call the departments that will be orienting large numbers of new staff each fall and ask to be included in their information seminars. Sometimes you will be asked to provide a brochure or handout, and sometimes they will ask you to staff a resource table at the event.

8. *Business cards for peer assistants.* In order to encourage as professional an image as possible in your peer assistants, consider making up general business cards for the program, with a space where assistants can write in their names when they make a contact with other students. This helps the patron remember whom they spoke to and advertises the program as a whole. It also gives the peer assistant prestige. Inexpensive business cards can be designed on a personal computer (see Appendix Three).

9. *Radio ads.* If your campus has a radio station that has many student listeners, consider placing radio ads. Some stations may even be willing to do a quick public service announcement for you. If there is a fee for the radio advertisement, the station should send its rate card to you ahead of time, along with information on listener demographics and statistics.

10. *Tee shirts and other usable take-away items.* For a relatively small amount of money one can produce a multicolor tee shirt that students will

gladly wear. The tee shirt serves as a walking billboard for your library program and promotes goodwill among your target students. Other similar products are easily ordered from many manufacturers throughout the country (see Table 8.1). Products such as pencils and pens embossed with the library's phone number and the program name, or stadium cups printed with a library graphic or the program logo and name help create goodwill toward the program. These promotion items can be toted to information fairs, handed out in bibliographic instruction classes, or given to students at the reference desk and on any appropriate occasion.

TRACING EFFECTIVENESS OF ADVERTISING VENUES

If you spend a significant amount of money on newspaper advertise-ments, it is a good idea to try to determine if the advertisements have been effective. Tracing the results of past advertisements helps you to adapt your advertising plan to current needs. There are several ways to judge how effective your ads have been:

- *Put coupons in ads when advertising your program's services.* Place a cut-out coupon in the body of the advertisement. Offer a freebie of some sort to students if they clip out the coupon and bring it in. At the end of the week in which the ad appeared, count the number of coupons that were turned in.
- *Ask students to mention ads when they call or drop in.* Within the body of an advertisement, tell students that mentioning your ad will earn them some sort of freebie. Keep a tally at the reference desk or other service point to which they are directed. At the end of the week count the number of mentions to determine whether or not the advertisement venue has been effective.

The problem with both of these evaluation methods is that many students will see the ad and remember the service later in the term, or simply won't clip the coupon or mention the ad when they do come in. If no one uses the coupon or mentions the ad, it may indicate that you need to reconsider before advertising again in that venue.

WHEN TO PLACE ADVERTISEMENTS

Timing the placement of advertisements is almost as important as preparing the copy. If the advertising budget is generous enough, two prime times should be considered: early in the semester, and around

Table 8.1
List of Suppliers

1. Rod Enterprises
    503 S. Park Avenue
    Tucson, Arizona 85719
    (602) 622-3522 / FAX (602) 622-2524

2. Advertisers Publishing Company
    P.O. Box 7010
    Ann Arbor, Michigan 48107-7010
    (313) 665-6171 / (800) 622-6171

3. JanWay Company
    11 Academy Road
    Cogan Station, PA 17728
    (800) 877-5242 / FAX (717) 494-1350

4. ALA Graphics
    American Library Association
    50 East Huron Street
    Chicago, Illinois 60611
    (800) 545-2433, press 8 or ext. 5048, 5049, 5050

5. Best Impressions Company
    348 North 30th Road
    P.O. Box 800
    LaSalle, Illinois 61301
    (815) 223-6263 / (800) 635-2378

6. National Women's History Project
    7738 Bell Road
    Windsor, CA 95492-8518
    (707) 838-6000 / FAX (707) 838-0478

7. WonderStorms
    1278 West Ninth Street
    Cleveland, Ohio 44113-1067
    (800) 321-1147 / FAX (216) 621-1366

8. Upstart
    32 East Avenue
    Hagerstown, Maryland 21740
    (800) 448-4887 / FAX (800) 448-5828

midterm time. If the budget is more modest, a decision must be made as to which time is more advantageous.

Early Advertisements

Advertising early in the semester has some advantages:

- When you place an early ad, you reach students early, while they are still impressionable.
- Early in the semester students have not been sidetracked by academic activities. Their minds are not yet occupied with tests and papers. You will also reach them before they become deeply involved in sporting events and other extracurricular activities.

Advertising early also has a few disadvantages:

- While not busy academically, early in the semester students are busy getting settled in, dropping and adding classes, and taking care of other housekeeping tasks. They may not be receptive to the information you provide.
- When they actually need the services and programs later in the term, they may have forgotten about them.

Midterm Advertisements

Advertising programs and services at midterm, when students need them most, has some advantages:

- The information about library services and programs is very fresh in students' minds, and they are more likely to act on it.
- The services now seem relevant to their needs, making it more likely that they will take advantage of them.

Obviously, it is best to advertise both at the beginning of the semester and close to the time of need if possible. The ad campaigns will complement one another to make the fullest impact on users.

INTERNAL P.R.: MARKETING TO OTHER LIBRARIES ON CAMPUS

In large, multilibrary systems we often forget that our library colleagues are the best promoters of our services. Communication between physically distant branches is not always easy. Make a special effort to visit branch libraries that have contact with your special target population to inform them about how your services will aid them in assisting these students. Asking branch heads to allow you to make a short presentation at their normally scheduled staff meetings; sending newsletters, brochures, and other literature to them via campus mail; and electronic messaging are effective means of getting the word out to library colleagues.

REFERENCES

Hamilton, Feona. *Infopromotion: Publicity and Marketing Ideas for the Information Profession*. Brookfield, Vt.: Gower, 1990.
Keiser, Barbie E., and Carol K. Galvin. *Marketing Library Services: A Nuts-and-Bolts Approach*. Sudbury, Mass.: Riverside Data, 1988.
Ostrow, Rona, and Sweetman R. Smith. *The Dictionary of Marketing*. New York: Fairchild Publications, 1988.
Weingand, Darlene E. *Marketing/Planning Library and Information Services*. Littleton, Colo.: Libraries Unlimited, 1987.
Wood, Elizabeth J., and Victoria L. Young. *Strategic Marketing for Libraries: A Handbook*. Westport, Conn.: Greenwood Press, 1988.

9

Program Evaluation

Evaluating library programs and services often feels painfully like taking an exam at the end of the school term. Staff members can become uncomfortable and nervous, and program planners themselves can find it tempting to deny the need to evaluate. Furthermore, evaluation of reference activities usually attempts to simplify and provide linear measures of something quite complex. Nevertheless, in spite of its potential inadequacies and drawbacks, evaluation is a necessary part of programming, especially when putting together something new. Concentrating on the benefits evaluation will bring to the program will help to lessen the test anxiety. Evaluation need not be difficult, and it should provide valuable information about the program and its directions, information that can be used to make the program even better.

This chapter outlines basic steps in evaluating a library program. Numerous resources elaborate further on each step in the process; several of the best are listed at the end of the chapter.

PLANNING FOR EVALUATION

Planning for evaluation should begin as early as possible. Some preliminary evaluation scheme should be ready before the program is actually implemented. You need to know how you expect to evaluate your program because this may affect its structure and will certainly affect some program activities. If the planning for evaluation is left until the end of a school year, for example, you may find you do not have the statistics you need or the names of clients to survey. Or you may be unable to reach clients who have already left campus. Actual assessment of the information collected may have to wait; the collection of the information cannot.

A search of the library literature will lead program planners to the extensive material on evaluation. How-to guides as well as examples of evaluation research are available from many institutions. This literature is a great jumping-off point for further developing your own ideas. Networking with librarians on other campuses or with other service providers on your own campus will also provide ideas on what to expect and how to proceed with the evaluation process.

In addition to deciding how to measure program activities and outcomes, planning includes identifying the tasks and who will execute them. It should also include a review of resources: staffing, finances, other support services such as mailroom services, and electronic resources like computers and software (the software available may constrain what data may be effectively analyzed).

Another element to consider is the target audience for the evaluation. If the evaluation report will be used by others outside of the immediate department, different kinds of information may need to be collected. Confer with everyone who will use the evaluation results to see what they would like to get from them.

Finally, be sure to set a timeline and deadlines for completion. The academic calendar and the fiscal calendar may both have a significant impact on the project.

IDENTIFYING DESIRED OUTCOMES

Revisit Goals and Objectives

Several first steps can be taken in starting an evaluation process. One critical first step is to review the goals and objectives established at the outset of the program to see whether they were met. The enabling objectives should have been written with measurement in mind. (For a discussion on writing goals and objectives, see Chapter Six.) For example, a stated objective may have been "to communicate information about the program to all first-year students on campus twice during the school year." Evaluation of this kind of objective is quite straightforward.

If no goals and objectives were specified initially, it is still possible to set them after the fact! The intent of the program needs to be articulated and recorded before evaluation research can proceed. It is also useful to set priorities in order to determine which activities or objectives should be first in line for evaluation (Hernon and McClure, 21).

Establish a Purpose for Evaluation

At the outset ask how and by whom the evaluation will be used. Several groups or individuals may make use of the evaluation: those who make funding decisions, the program coordinator, and the library development office, for example. Some of them may even have extra-library publicity in mind.

The purpose of the evaluation may be formulated as a set of specific questions the researcher wishes to answer. For example:

- How successful was the program? Did it accomplish its objectives or achieve unanticipated outcomes?
- Are the objectives appropriate?
- What changes might be necessary or beneficial to the program?
- What kind of funding is necessary to continue or expand the program? How appropriate was the allocation?
- What are the staff development needs?
- What other services might be necessary (such as a series of instructional handouts)?
- How can we better communicate with the target audience of the program?

Another way to think about the goals of the evaluation is to use five general measurement concepts to help clarify the direction the evaluation should take (Hernon and McClure, 5). The evaluation is to determine:

1. The extensiveness of service, such as amount of service per population served;
2. The effectiveness of service, or how well objectives or user needs are met;
3. The efficiency of service, or appropriateness of resource allocation;
4. The cost-effectiveness of service, or how well objectives are met based on costs;
5. The cost-benefit of service, or the benefits derived from a service compared to the cost of the service.

An evaluation cannot realistically cover all of these concepts. Each requires different kinds of information and research. Furthermore, there is little reason to expend resources answering questions about which no one cares. Set priorities to help determine which questions or desired outcomes to pursue.

The evaluation plan may have one objective or several. The objective may also change from year to year. Awareness of how you plan to use the evaluation will help determine the measures and methods used. For example, the primary purpose of the evaluation may be to request continued or additional funding. Demonstrating that the program met its objectives will be useful, but only if those in charge of funding sources are fully supportive of those objectives. In some cases, an evaluation of the extensiveness of service might be more convincing, as might a cost-benefit analysis.

SELECTING APPROPRIATE METHODS

Once you have some idea of the goals of the evaluation and the resources available to support the evaluation process, the next step is to determine the methods appropriate to achieving those goals. Evaluative research is generally divided into two categories, quantitative and qualitative. Within those broad categories are many types of research tools, such as unobtrusive tests, surveys, participant observation, interviews, document analysis, and telephone interviews. Each will offer different kinds of information to meet different research needs.

Basic Methods

Evaluation can be a very creative process. However, a new method does not need to be devised each time an evaluation is conducted. Several commonly used methods are described briefly below. These methods are not mutually exclusive, and it can even be advantageous to combine several, for example, following up on focus group discussions with the distribution of a general survey. Ideally, the strengths and weaknesses of each method may be offset by using multiple approaches.

General surveys. This would be a survey of the entire target group at the very least. If the targeted user group is black and Latino freshmen, for example, a survey that includes all freshmen provides comparative information. This wider view can provide a picture of the clientele or pool of potential users and how their opinions or perceptions compare to nonminority freshmen, feedback on what services they would like to see, how they use (or do not use) the library, and so forth. A broad survey such as this can help the evaluator answer questions about program visibility, program effectiveness, and appropriateness of objectives. And a survey of those who have used special library programs can be embedded within the more general survey.

The primary problems with general surveys are the resources they absorb—a relatively large number of questionnaires to print and mail, for example—and the notoriously poor response rate they usually receive. The conscientious will reply, as will those with very strong opinions. Further, because respondents will be self-selected, they will probably not be a representative sample of the target group pool. Finally, in order to keep the survey length manageable and to improve response rate, limit the number of questions. It may also be necessary to confine the survey to structured or multiple choice questions rather than open-ended questions that allow respondents to express themselves in their own words and at some length. Structured questions restrict the respondents' answers by limiting their choices to a set of possibilities predetermined by the researcher. Obviously, this constrains what respondents can tell you. Nevertheless, many survey respondents actually prefer limited choices to open-ended questions because the survey can be completed faster. Researchers often prefer structured responses, too, because they are much easier to code and handle statistically. Surveys can combine both types of questions, but if too many questions require written answers, many respondents will choose to skip them, or to skip the questionnaire altogether.

A general survey may provide a good statistical picture of the target population as well as of the program users and user satisfaction. It can also retrieve some qualitative information through the inclusion of open-ended questions. A disadvantage of this kind of survey is that it can become lengthy and complicated, thus reducing response rates.

User surveys. Presumably this group would be considerably smaller than the group reached by a more general survey and thus would normally require fewer resources. It may also be possible to send more follow-up surveys and increase the response rate. It may be effective to make a pitch to users in a cover letter noting their special status as program users and how important their responses will be to the continued success of the program, thereby increasing the chance they will respond. While a smaller, more select survey may allow more room for open-ended questions, surveys still remain somewhat impersonal.

Interviews. Interviews of program users or representatives of the target audience can provide much more in-depth answers to the same questions that might be asked on a survey. Respondents are better able to elaborate on their answers. Interviewers can clarify questions that individuals may not understand. More of an exchange takes place between evaluator and respondent. Also, the evaluator selects the respondents, rather than having to rely on self-selection. Interviews can be useful as a pretest for a broader questionnaire.

Interviews, however, are extremely time-consuming. The number of respondents will likely be small. And it is also easy to lose consistency in questioning from one interview to the next, especially if more than one interviewer is involved.

Focus groups. Focus groups can be an excellent way to stimulate focused discussion and provide in-depth views on issues. They are similar to interviews, but the exchange is now between a larger number of people who can build upon each other's comments and ideas. Focus groups do not have to be expensive, though they tend to be time-consuming. They are an excellent way to follow up on survey responses or to develop survey questions (Widdows et al., 354).

A group, though, can be intimidating to some participants, and those with extreme points of view may fail to speak up. An individual may also try to dominate discussion. Also, outcomes of the focus group may not be generalizable to the larger group.

Observation. Observation—obtrusive, unobtrusive, or participative— allows the evaluator to view the program and its participants in action. In unobtrusive observation, the observer is not known to any of those being observed, though employees and patrons may be notified that observation may be taking place. In obtrusive observation the observer is not involved in the activity, but is known and visible to the participants. In participant observation the observer becomes part of the activity, for example, observing a peer counselor while both the observer and the counselor work at the reference desk. Observation is particularly useful in tracking interactions between staff and patrons and might also help to shed light on what other services or program changes might be needed.

Observation does not provide a complete picture, however, even in regard to the questions it addresses. It cannot show, for example, how the patron viewed the outcome of his or her contact with the library staff member. That would require a follow-up survey or interview. Known observation also makes many people—staff and patrons alike—very nervous, while also raising ethical questions, such as concern about fairness to the staff member and the role of unobtrusive observation in employment decisions.

Experimentation. Experimentation, such as actually testing the library skills of program users, can produce interesting and valuable data. Evaluators can test program users and similar nonusers, for example, in order to independently assess program impact and effectiveness. The evaluator does not have to rely exclusively on the respondent's self-reported assessment of his own skill development.

This method, too, is labor-intensive. Setting up the study and finding subjects may be difficult. It could also become costly, especially if the subjects are remunerated in some way. In particular, it would take time to identify a control group that has characteristics similar to the test group. It is also hard to know what the subjects knew before participating in the program unless they were tested prior to participation.

Using Statistics

Numbers have a certain appeal. Because they may seem to be definitive, authoritative, and unbiased, arguing against numerical results is often difficult. That is why a statistical analysis is often an attractive method of evaluation.

Few people have strong backgrounds in statistics. Simple statistics, such as numbers of people contacted via publicity, or percentage of reference questions answered by peer counselors, are often quite adequate. For more sophisticated statistical needs, a researcher may wish to seek assistance. Faculty or students from the sociology or the statistics department, or from the nearest library school, for example, may be willing to help for a small fee, course credit, the opportunity to write an article, or perhaps even gratis. A number of books also offer detailed guidance to library researchers interested in statistics. (See the list of resources at the end of this chapter.) Keep in mind that the researcher is unlikely to get a database of sufficient size and consistency to make complex analysis feasible. It may well not be worth the effort, as few readers of the results of the evaluation would understand the analysis.

Although numbers give the appearance of objectivity, bias does creep into statistical research, through the questions that are asked or in the way they are asked. Bias can also appear when determining which figures to use and which to ignore. Finally, the interpretation of those figures can certainly produce bias. It is important to keep in mind that quantitative analysis cannot answer all questions, nor can it answer them fully. For example, in a test of library users you may be able to determine how many questions are answered incorrectly, but statistics will not show *why* those questions were answered incorrectly (Shavit, 237). As comforting as numbers can be, evaluators should consider using qualitative evaluation as well.

Nonstatistical Evaluation

Though quantitative evaluation can offer useful information about how a program is operating, qualitative evaluation may help to complete the picture. As with quantitative evaluation, the type of information required will determine the kind of qualitative research to be done. Interviewing program users may help determine how well the program is meeting its objectives. Observation may show areas where staff development is needed. An open-ended question or two on a more structured survey may reveal information about what innovations students would like to see. Qualitative research can help to round out the statistical picture as well as answer questions that you did not think to ask.

DESIGNING THE EVALUATION

Referring to the burgeoning literature on evaluation for descriptions of other evaluations will spark ideas for design plans. (See Appendix Two.) Designs should be as simple as possible to meet the needs of the evaluation and to address the interests of those who will read the evaluation. Costs in time, money, and other resources should be estimated well in advance of implementing the evaluation.

One simple and usually quick way to document respondents' evaluations is to ask them to write a letter answering particular questions, such as the following:

- How often did you see or refer someone to the service?
- What would you consider the most important aspects of the program?
- What is the biggest problem of the program?
- What about the service would you change? What would you add?

Other staff members are usually glad to help out, particularly if they see some benefit to themselves or to their students in keeping the program going. If, however, they lack time to write a letter of evaluation, the program coordinator may conduct and write up a brief interview which covers the key questions and ask the other staff members to sign or otherwise confirm the evaluation's contents. Documentation is important. You may get daily praise for the program by word of mouth, but when it comes to a formal presentation, those word-of-mouth evaluations will bear little weight.

Users, employees, and co-workers can do the same kind of write-up. This gives the evaluator a useful set of documents to analyze and summarize in a final report.

When planning the questions remember that most respondents tend to express satisfaction with library services in part because they do not know what else might be possible within the library. There may be ways to get around this. For example, describe specifically what you think they should have gotten out of the program: not "did you learn enough about the online catalog," but "on a scale of one to five with five being 'very well,' after meeting with the peer counselor, how well can you find material on a desired subject in the online catalog," or "which of the following library resources did you use for your last research project," followed by a list of items that peer counselors are trained to introduce to other students. Keep yes/no questions to a minimum. If you would like ideas for program enhancements, perhaps suggesting a few possibilities will stimulate further thoughts by the respondents.

EVALUATING THE EVALUATION

This may seem to be simply going too far, but the evaluation itself does in fact need to be evaluated to make sure that the questions are understandable and that the design will retrieve the information required. In a survey, for example, take time to pretest the questions. The pretest helps identify problem questions: questions that may be ambiguous or otherwise poorly worded, questions that use jargon, questions that are unnecessary, or questions that generate information that you do not want. For example, a library user survey at the University of Michigan which included a section on "demographic data" listed the category "Native American," intending to identify those of American Indian heritage. But the large number of people who checked that box was far out of proportion to the campus population of Native Americans. It was finally determined that some respondents interpreted that category to mean that they had been born in the United States. Obviously, responses for that category had to be discounted. A pretest would probably have identified this problem, and the category could have been designated "Native American/American Indian."

Surveys should always be pretested on those who will accurately represent the intended respondents. In other words, student staff members or others very familiar with the library (or familiar with library jargon like "stacks" or "serials" that may have slipped into the survey) should be excluded. Pretest surveys on a random group of patrons in the library, in a dorm or group of dorms, in the student union or other campus gathering place. A faculty member may also be willing to let his or her class act as your pretest group.

If an interview is planned, be sure to review the questions, making certain that they clearly ask what is intended. Watch for jargon, complexity, double-edged questions, and ambiguity. Try the questions out on a representative respondent—or several—if possible.

The process of evaluating the evaluation need not take long and will reduce the possibility that serious problems will appear after the research is completed. The time spent will be well worth it.

ADMINISTERING THE EVALUATION

Surveys

Administering a campus-wide survey may mean no more than stuffing and labeling envelopes addressed to students and putting them in campus mail. A campus data center, registrar's office, or other administrative unit should be able to provide the names and mailing labels for little or no cost. If surveying only those who have actually used the service, you can generate printed mailing labels from your own database if one has been maintained. Otherwise, student assistants or other desk workers may label or address and stuff envelopes during slow service periods.

Include in the mailing a letter describing the survey and its goals, assuring anonymity, and explaining why the respondent should complete the survey, how to return it, and whom to contact with questions or comments. A return envelope will increase the likelihood that the survey will be returned. If the resources are available, include a small thank-you gift, such as a pencil stamped with the program name, a bookmark, or a certificate for a free packet of information (redeemable at the library, of course!).

If you have a master list of respondents or a second set of mailing labels, it is very useful to code outgoing surveys. Number respondents on the master list and mark the survey with the corresponding number. When surveys are returned, check off the name of the respondents, or simply cross off or discard the numbered address label in the second set. When a follow-up copy of the survey is sent, second copies will not go out to those who have already returned them. This will save money and time for the researcher.

This may seem an obsession with the anonymity promise, but at no time is a name actually attached to a particular response or survey. Also, in the reporting of the results, names will not be used. If respondents express concern about this procedure, the researcher could have a second person who would not be reading the forms actually check them in. This can be explained explicitly up front or to only those respondents who express concern over the coding.

Interviews

Other methods, such as interviews and focus groups, often take considerable time to set up. One-on-one interviews can become very time-consuming for the evaluator, though they are easier to set up than focus groups because there are fewer schedules to coordinate. One way to reduce the burden on one researcher is to recruit others to assist in interviews. These assistants will most likely be other library staff members, but may also include graduate or undergraduate students or faculty from appropriate departments. All the researchers should have the same set of questions to ask or areas to cover, and should reach an agreement on how the interview will be recorded and reported. A script of questions does not mean inflexibility, but assures that key concerns are addressed, along with anything else the respondent may wish to bring up. Audio or video recording assures the researcher of having the full content of the interview, although some respondents may be unwilling to be taped. However, listening to and transcribing such tapes is an extremely tedious task. If mechanical recording is not used, a second person should take notes, freeing the interviewer to keep things moving. Notes should be detailed and use the respondent's own words as much as possible. A note-taker from outside of the library may be less likely to screen the responses unconsciously, and therefore may provide more accurate notes on the interview. The option pursued will, of course, depend on the researcher's specific needs and on the resources available.

Focus Groups

Focus groups of students may need to meet during odd hours, such as early evening or weekends. An incentive may help improve attendance (pizza or donuts work wonders). An off-site location, such as a dormitory or a local restaurant, may also be more attractive than the library. The location must be comfortable and convenient for participants, quiet enough to allow the recorder to be accurate, and arranged in a manner to promote discussion.

A script of questions can direct discussion but should remain flexible so that other issues are allowed to come up as well (Widdows et al.,

354). The interactive nature of the focus group is one of its major advantages. The moderator must not impose a rigid structure on the group discussion. As with interviews, the monitoring and recording of focus group activities will depend on the researcher as well as on the resources available.

A trial focus group may provide some ideas for questions. General questions may be very useful just to get the discussion going: for example, "What do you like least about the library?" Other questions might specifically address what students know about the peer counseling program or other library services, how they use the library, and so forth.

ANALYZING RESPONSES

If data have been collected, the statistics reported do not have to be complex; in fact, it is probably best to keep them as simple as possible, while meeting the needs of the evaluation plan. Also, keep in mind who is going to read the final report as well as how much time and energy the evaluator has available to put into the final product. The statistics can be simple percentages, such as the percentage of the target population that reported having heard of the program, the percentage of users that reported satisfaction with the program, or the percentage of users who returned for further help. These kinds of numbers are fairly easy to calculate even without statistical software. A large number of software packages, too, can accept data and rapidly calculate required results, and even draw charts and tables. Some are fairly simple to use. (See the appendix to this chapter for a list of some software packages.)

Interview or focus group transcripts can be quantified and numerically evaluated as well by counting how often particular issues were mentioned by respondents. Or topics may be clustered in order to identify broad themes (Widdows et al., 355) and depth of feeling about the issues.

REPORTING RESULTS

Program evaluators should always prepare a written document reporting the results of the evaluation. Even if the evaluation is conducted by the program organizer with no intention of sharing it with others, or presented only orally to library administrators or to another audience, a written document stands as a record of what was accomplished for further reference. If nothing else, it can help the program coordinator to remember what did and did not work when the time comes to run another evaluation.

The evaluation should be written with the target reader in mind. If it is to be part of a pitch for funding, the language should be that of the administrators or outside agency receiving the document. The "right" language can make the document more credible to the reader. Unless the primary readers will be librarians, avoid technical library terminology or any other jargon with which the reader might not be familiar (for example, the language of statisticians is a mystery to many). Whoever the readers are, the language should be straightforward and clear. Charts, tables, and other illustrations may provide a simpler presentation of information (especially statistical information) than does text, though some text is certainly necessary to tie illustrations together and to meet the needs of those who prefer not to deal with graphic presentations.

The evaluation report should cover the following (Hernon and McClure, 202–3):

- context of evaluation, background, and description of program;
- what the evaluation intends to accomplish;
- procedures or methods and justification for methods chosen;
- findings, probably in a summary format (it is rarely useful and usually overwhelming to include all of the raw data);
- conclusions based on findings; and
- specific recommendations.

When drawing up recommendations, give some thought to their implications. A recommendation to expand a program should clearly state what that would mean: larger staff, more hours, more locations, more services, and so on. It might also address the issue of costs and describe in some preliminary fashion plans to assess program changes.

To the final report should be appended copies of materials used in the evaluation, such as a copy of a survey, texts of answers to open-ended questions, a list of questions used in interviews, a list of documents reviewed, and so on. An executive summary preceding the report gives it a professional, finished appearance and also aids those who will not have time to read through the entire document. The executive summary, no more than a page or two in length, is essentially an abstract of the document that follows. Finally, if there is time, a literature review can help the reader place the evaluation in a broader context and may offer a comparative view.

IMPLEMENTING RECOMMENDATIONS
AS APPROPRIATE

Evaluation usually implies the possibility of change, however minor. You may determine, for example, that you can expand the program to three times its size and serve many more people. Alternatively, overly ambitious goals may need to be reduced. Or the program may simply take a new direction.

Some recommendations may not be at the evaluator's level of responsibility, in which case further documentation or other follow-up material may be needed to convince those at higher levels to implement changes.

ADDITIONAL CONSIDERATIONS

The steps presented above are not hard and fast rules but one approach to the essential process of evaluation. The person responsible for conducting the evaluation should tailor it to meet the specific needs and abilities of the program and department. Outlining a process, then breaking it into steps and tackling each step one at a time, will make what might otherwise seem a formidable task easier to accomplish.

The intent of evaluation is the improvement of existing services. To accomplish this may require changing the evaluation process at some point depending on changes in the program, the community, or the institution. Of course, frequent changes in the evaluation plan may result in the loss of the ability to make comparisons over time. Nevertheless, it is important to keep in mind that a program is never locked into a structure and should be flexible enough to change in all aspects—including evaluation.

RESOURCES FOR LIBRARY RESEARCH
AND EVALUATION

This has been a very brief examination of program evaluation techniques. There is a considerable literature on the subject of evaluation in libraries, and more appears every year. A literature review of relevant case studies will provide valuable information to the librarian planning an evaluation. In addition, a number of general works on the topic are available. A list of useful works on library evaluation and research follows.

Bradley, Jana. *Improving Written Communication in Libraries*. Chicago: American Library Association, 1988.

Cooper, Alan. *An Introduction to Statistics for Librarians*. Loughborough, Leicestershire: Centre for Library and Information Studies, Loughborough University, 1982.

Hernon, Peter, and Charles R. McClure. *Evaluation and Library Decision Making*. Norwood, N.J.: Ablex Publishing, 1990.

Hernon, Peter, et al. *Statistics for Library Decision Making*. Norwood, N.J.: Ablex Publishing, 1989.

Powell, Ronald. *Basic Research Methods for Librarians*. Norwood, N.J.: Ablex Publishing, 1991.

Simpson, I. S. *Basic Statistics for Librarians*. London: Clive Bingley, 1983.

Slater, Margaret, ed. *Research Methods in Library and Information Studies*. London: Library Association, 1990.

Westbrook, Lynn. *Qualitative Evaluation Methods for Reference Services: An Introductory Manual*. Washington, D.C.: Association of Research Libraries, 1989.

REFERENCES

Hernon, Peter, and Charles McClure. *Evaluation and Library Decision Making*. Norwood, N.J.: Ablex Publishing, 1990.

Shavit, David. "Qualitative Evaluation of Reference Service." *Reference Librarian*, no. 11 (Fall/Winter 1984).

Widdows, Richard, Tia Hensler, and Marlaya Wyncott. "The Focus Group: A Method for Assessing Users' Evaluation of Library Service." *College and Research Libraries* 54, no. 4 (July 1991), 354.

APPENDIX: STATISTICAL ANALYSIS SOFTWARE

These statistical packages were selected for their ease of use. They will also do basic statistical analysis as well as more complex analysis. Scores of other software programs are available, as well as numerous directories of software programs. Some sources are listed below.

FASTAT (Macintosh)

Producer: SYSTAT Inc.
             1800 Sherman Ave.
             Evanston, IL 60201
             708-864-5670

Price (1991): $195

STATVIEW II (Macintosh)

Producer: Abacus Concepts, Inc.
             1984 Bonita Ave.
             Berkeley, CA 94704
             415-540-1949

Price (1991): $495

SPSS/PC+ (PC and compatibles)

Producer: SPSS Inc.
             444 North Michigan Ave.
             Chicago, IL 60611
             312-329-3300
             800-543-6609

Price (1991): $395

SYSTAT (Macintosh and PC and compatibles)

Producer: SYSTAT Inc.
             1800 Sherman Ave.
             Evanston, IL 60201
             708-864-5670

Price (1991): $595 for SYSTAT only
                $795 for SYSTAT and
                SYGRAPH

Sources of information:
Datapro Directory of Microcomputer Software. Delran, NJ: McGraw-Hill, 1991.
The Software Encyclopedia 1991. New Providence, NJ: Bowker, 1991.
Software Reviews On File. New York: Facts on File, Inc., 1985-

Appendix 1

Training Plans and Exercises

REFERENCE DESK TRAINING PLANS
for
Selected Staff and Student Assistants
Undergraduate Library
The University of Michigan

Training Taskforce:
Harold Tuckett (chair), Bob Diaz
Darlene Nichols, Linda TerHaar, March 1989
Updated: Barbara Hoppe, May 1991

TABLE OF CONTENTS

I. CONTEXT

There are three groups of students who work at the UGL Reference Desk:

1) Reference Assistants: These are paid graduate students in the School of Information and Library Science at UM. When hired they must have had or be taking the basic reference course. They work a minimum of six hours a week on the desk. Generally we hire only those who are willing to stay at least one year. When fully trained they are allowed to cover the desk entirely alone; much of their work includes staffing the desk on weekends with no back-up.

2) Field Experience Interns: These are unpaid graduate students in the School of Information and Library Science at UM. They do a variety of jobs in exchange for class credit. Most of them request desk duty. Those who can give the minimum six hours and who have had, or are taking, the basic reference course, are allowed to work on the desk. In addition, they frequently have projects in other areas such as collection development, online services, or BI. They stay for only one term. They never work alone since part of the educational component of their time includes the opportunity to work with, observe, and get feedback from the full-time and professional staff.

3) Peer Information Counselors: These are paid undergraduates, primarily juniors and seniors with some sophomores, from all fields of study. In addition to working on the reference desk, many of them serve in the Academic Resource Center where they teach word processing to anyone who asks for their assistance. They may stay for anywhere from a single term to three years. They never work alone on the desk as they are expected to refer some questions. A special component of their work is to provide one-to-one contact for any patron who needs someone to spend more time on a question than is usually possible at the busy desk. For example, someone who is having difficulty locating a book may be referred to a PIC student so that the PIC student can actually leave the floor and walk the patron through the search process. On the other hand, PIC students are trained to refer patrons with complex or less common questions to the reference assistants, interns, and reference staff with whom they work whenever they have any hesitation about the fullness or quality of their answer. PIC students are the mainstay of the PIC program, a minority student support program at UGL. They are therefore often involved in a variety of projects. Nevertheless, they tend to average at least 6 hours a week on the desk, often more.

  The Coordinator for PIC adjusts the training program somewhat based on the needs and experience of the PIC trainees. The schedule, methods, and timing may therefore vary for those students.

In addition to these groups of students, certain self-selected full-time staff are considered for desk work. People who have been with UGL full-time for two or more years, have the permission of their supervisor, and have a strong public service attitude when working with undergraduates are considered for reference desk training when they request the opportunity. They work at least four and no more than six hours per week on the reference desk. They serve as back-up in case no full-time reference staff member or School of Information and Library Studies (SILS) student can work the desk during the regular weekday hours. They never work weekends or nights. In general, they serve during busy times with a full-time reference staff member. The advantages for these staff members are those of personal growth and variation in duties. The advantage for the reference staff is the creation of a trained pool of emergency back-up help. The advantage to the public is the contact with people who have an in-depth knowledge of another major service point in the library.

The training program described herein is designed to prepare students and selected staff to work on a busy reference desk covering all fields with a clientele composed, primarily, of undergraduates. In addition to an online catalog (based on the NOTIS system with keyword/boolean features), staff work with *Reader's Guide* on CD Rom and *InfoTrac*. The UGL reference desk is staffed by six librarians and one para-professional. During the school year hours are generally: Monday to Thursday from 9 to 5 and 6 to 10; Friday 9-5; Saturday 10-5; and Sunday 1-5 and 6-10.

DESK OBSERVATION GUIDELINES

During the training period you will be observing reference staff in their work on the desk. These guidelines should help make that observation easier and more useful. When in doubt about anything, just ask.

When Do I Start Observing?

As soon as you have finished your first training session you are welcome to begin observation.

How Do I Schedule It?

You don't. Just show up whenever you feel like it. You may find it most useful to observe during the times you will later be working on the desk. If you show up and find too many others also observing, just talk to them about finding another time.

What Do I Wear?

If possible, wear what you would wear when working on the desk. So long as you are neat and clean you will be fine.

What Do I Do If Someone Asks Me A Question?

Refer the patron to the person who is on the desk. Do not try to answer questions yourself unless you are absolutely certain that you (1) understand the full question and (2) have the full answer. Telling someone how to find the water fountain is fine. Telling someone how to read the call number location chart or find a dictionary can be more complex than it seems. Gradually you will learn how to move through a reference interview well enough to know that you do indeed understand the full question.

Do I Wear A Badge?

Probably. A badge lets people know that you are part of the library staff. If they read it, they will also know that you are observing or in training.

When Do I Stop Observing and Start Working On The Desk?

After your last training session and after your exercises have been completed, then you can move from observation to desk work. You will know when you are ready. When you move to desk work be sure to change your badge and to let the people you are working with know that you are making the change.

How Do I Work With The People I Am Observing?

Introduce yourself. Read the desk log. Follow the staff member around and watch. Ask questions about how the interview was conducted, how the reference tools were chosen, and how the material was taught. Take notes if you like. If things are quiet then work on your exercises; ask for assistance on them if you like.

What If My Observing Appears To Bother A Patron?

Stop. Back off. If it seems acceptable, explain that you are in training for desk work and are therefore observing the reference staff member. Emphasize that you are not observing the patron at all. If in doubt, though, just stop the observation on that patron.

BASIC INFORMATION FORM

This information will help us reach you in case there are any changes in schedule about which you should be notified. The information at the bottom will help us focus your training and the follow-up, subject-oriented sessions to your needs and skills. Please complete this right now and return it to your instructor.

Name_____ Phone _____

Address _____electronic mail account

Is there any place we can leave a message for you?_____

Each term we try to put out a list of names and phone numbers in each job family (i.e., Reference Assistants, Interns, and PIC staff). Since you are required to change hours only with members of your own job family, this list is usually helpful when you are searching for someone to exchange hours with you. The list only goes to desk staff. Would you like your name, electronic mail status, and number on that list?　　　YES　　NO
****
Reference Assistant/Intern/PIC staff member/Other:_____

Have you worked in a library before? If so, where? Doing what?

_____

_____

What is your educational status and background? Junior in English or SILS 2nd semester student with a BA in German? SILS students: list all reference courses, past and present.

_____

_____

Do you have any skills, interests, or other experiences which might be relevant to this work?

_____

_____

What are you most interested in getting out of this training? Is there anything you want detailed instruction on?

_____

_____

What most interests you about doing this work? _____

_____

LIST OF MAIN POINTS

Dress policy: dress professionally; standards do not relax on weekends, evenings, or summer hours.

Staffing: required to make switches within your own job family; notify your supervisor ASAP of any problems.

Reference Service Policy: direct personal assistance to all users; teaching library.

Slow Times: always watch for patrons who are hesitant to interrupt; do library work; avoid socializing.

Telephone service: in-person patrons have priority; let the answering machine handle people who call; if you answer the phone at least take the question; call back if need be; do not do more research for phone patrons than for in-person patrons.

TIMECARD INSTRUCTIONS

When beginning and ending each work shift, student assistants punch in and out on a time clock using long white cards. The clock is located in the main floor staff lounge area. Blank timecards are on the shelf by the time clock.

You should use a new card for each week, beginning with Sunday. At the top of the card put your name and the date of the following Saturday. Keep the card in the card rack with the other Reference Assistants' cards.

If you do project work at home, indicate on your timecard the date and number of hours worked at home.

At the end of the week, bracket each day's punches. If you are totaling you own timecard, indicate each day's total in hours and tenths of hours. Six minutes=1/10 hour. Total the week in hours and tenths of hours.

Timecards must go in on time in order for you to be paid on time. If you run into problems, contact your supervisor.

NOTE: For College Work Study Student Assistants
1. Use ballpoint pen.
2. Be sure to sign the card!!!!!
3. Check the College Work Study box in the upper right-hand corner.

II. TRAINING OUTLINE AND SCHEDULE

I. Introduction to UGL: Two and one half hours.
   A. UGL's function as a teaching library
   B. Basics for all student employees
      1. Timecards
      2. Student Employee Handbook
      3. Housekeeping for rest of training period
   C. Tours of UGL and Graduate Library
WHEN_____ WHERE_____

II. Orientation to the reference desk: Two hours.
   A. Policies and Procedures Manual
   B. Reference desk checklist
   C. Commonly asked questions
   D. Emergency procedures
WHEN_____ WHERE_____

III. Access to the collection: Two and one half hours.
   A. Books (known items)
   B. Serials (known items)
   C. Books (unknown items)
   D. Serials (unknown items)
WHEN_____ WHERE_____

IV. Reference interview and search strategy: Two hours.
   A. Review reference philosophy
   B. Reference interview
   C. Search strategy
WHEN_____ WHERE_____

V. Basic reference tools: Two hours.
   A. Fact tools
   B. Finding tools
WHEN_____ WHERE_____

VI. Automated services: Two hours.
   A. Overview of UGL automated services
   B. How to handle all end-user services
WHEN_____ WHERE_____

Further Training:
These sessions are offered after the basic training has been completed and
everyone is working at the desk. Each session reviews tools, relevant search
strategies, and other concerns (such as proper referrals) by subject:
biographical, literary criticism, statistics, political science, science, education,
business. Each session is about 30 to 50 minutes. These will be scheduled at
a later date.

III. INSTRUCTOR'S OUTLINES FOR SESSIONS ONE TO SIX

SESSION I

Introduction to The Library

A. UGL's function as a teaching library
Head of the library or Reference Coordinator speaks to the group.
Define purpose of reference in this library and role of this library on
campus. Emphasize service orientation of this staff. Discuss
confidentiality and ethics.

Followed by discussion of service attitudes. Discuss such questions as
the following: Have they worked in libraries before? What was the
service attitude there? As patrons, how would they define the ideal
service attitude?

Also cover ground rules for observing at the desk, such as wearing a
name tag and how to handle it when patrons ask questions they can not
answer.

Teaching Method: Address with discussion.
Application: Observe it in action on the desk and do some observation.

B. Basics for all student employees and interns

1. Timecards (paid student assistants only)
How to fill them out. Where they are. Where to go with problems.
Warning about having them in late.
2. Student Employee Handbook
Explain organization of UGL with various departments. Rules for
dress, working in public areas, and rules of behavior while on the
job. How to call in sick and arrange for switching hours.
Encourage employees to report any incidents of harassment.
3. Housekeeping for rest of training period
Have everyone fill out and return the Basic Information Form. If
necessary, schedule remaining training periods. Distribute Outline
of Training Plan and answer any questions they may have.

Teaching Method: Lecture highlighting handbook points with
question period.
Application: Actually use timecard; read handbook.

C. Tours of UGL and other important libraries

UGL: Use the checklist. Be sure to check off items as you go, note
any difficulties or questions, and add any points you think need to be
included in future sessions.

Graduate Library: Explain how to get into and out of that complex building from both directions. Might actually have them split up and try to meet in the card catalog area with those who know leading those who don't know. Visit the main public service points: main circulation, Interlibrary Loan, reference, microform room, serials, government documents, and the Map Library. Emphasize the services offered at each stop and the best way to direct someone to locate each stop. Give them copies of the Guide to the Graduate Library.

Teaching Method: Tour with introductions to as many Undergraduate Library staff as possible as well as key Graduate Library staff.

Application: Expected to find their way around and be able to ask questions of various staff members, complete observation, and begin answering minimal directional questions. They should also be encouraged to take one of the self-guided tours.

Assignment: Read the Student Employees' Handbook.
Desk Work: Have them start observing.
Handouts: Student Employees' Handbook; Training Outline and Schedule; first timecard; guide to Graduate Library; self-guided tour; Basic Information Form; observation guidelines; syllabus for field experience students.

SESSION II

Orientation to the Reference Desk

A. Reference desk checklist
   1. Walk them through each of the sections of the checklist.
   2. Walk them through the opening and closing procedures if at all possible; also have them schedule a time to do this on their own under the supervision of a full-time reference staff member.

   Teaching Method: Demonstration; have them actually do as many things as possible. Be sure every student takes active part. Consider having different people work on different things rather than all waiting turns for one item. If time allows, repeat key sections such as where to find instructions for bringing up all computers.
   Application: Encourage them to do as many of the checklist items as possible during their coming observation sessions. Suggest that they actually schedule a time just so they can open or close the desk. Suggest that they try replacing ribbons, fixing paper, finding specific items in the file drawers and bins, etc.

B. Emergency procedures
   1. Introduce their role during emergencies. Be sure that anyone who might ever work alone, particularly on weekends, is completely current on all emergency procedures and knows where the

emergency notebook is kept. Give them the copies of the
Emergency Procedures handout.

C. Commonly asked questions
    1. Introduce the handout on commonly asked questions. Give them a
       few minutes to look it over; answer any questions. Encourage
       them to review this when they are on the desk observing.

Teaching Method: This will probably be something which they
must do on their own, due to time constraints. If possible, ask a few
of the questions, then see if anyone can provide even a partial answer.
Try to encourage peer teaching by suggesting they team up during
observation stints and ask each other the questions. Be sure people
know the "why" behind each answer or at least feel quite free to ask for
it when working with a staff member.
Application: Point out that these are the first questions they can really
answer on the desk and that they should begin looking for
opportunities to do so.

D. Policies and Procedures Manual
    1. Hand out copies of the main points of the manual and explain that,
       while they should be familiar with the entire manual, these sections
       are particularly important.

Teaching Method: Brief introduction followed by question period.
This should be followed by each student, on their own, actively
moving through the process from finding the procedure in the manual
to exiting the building and/or moving to the basement. Be sure they
can locate flashlight, procedures, and each area for which they are
responsible in times of emergency.
Application: Point out that a fire or tornado drill is possible at any
time. Encourage them to review the procedures at the desk with
whomever they next observe.

Assignment: Have them take the self-guided tour on their own if they
                have not already done so; self-scheduled. Have them
                review outline of Manual, reference checklist,
                opening/closing procedures, emergency procedures.

Desk Work: Have them continue observing on the desk. Allow them
                to answer directional questions if they feel ready.

Handouts: UGL Reference Area Checklist; Opening and Closing the
                Reference Desk; emergency procedures; Commonly
                Asked Questions.

SESSION III

Access to the Collection

A. Books (known items): Each tool offers some information not available elsewhere.
   1. Online Catalog: comprehensive coverage of all acquisitions since 1975; retrospective conversion virtually complete. Teach them basics of author and title searching. Show basics of doing an authority search and a call number search in staff mode.
   2. Card catalog: UGL special files such as tapes and plot summaries only; GL's is comprehensive but it closed in 1988.
   3. Research Libraries Information Network contains everything we've cataloged since 1975; expensive to use now so only use it for verification and other searching when MIRLYN (online catalog) will not suffice. Point out again where to find search instructions when at desk. Have people do at least one MIRLYN search.

   Teaching Method: Lecture demonstration with everyone expected to conduct at least one search in each system.
   Application: Access exercise and some desk work.

B. Serials (known items): Each tool offers some unique information.
   1. Take them into room 126 and explain its arrangement and rules.
   2. MIRLYN: comprehensive; does not include complete information about individual issues.
   3. Show how to interpret hook-to-holdings screens.
   4. SSR: referral; individual issues.

   Teaching Method: Lecture demonstration with everyone expected to conduct at least one search in MIRLYN.
   Application: Access exercise and some desk work.

C. Books (unknown items): Use subject searching and keyword searching.
   1. LCSH
   2. MESH
   3. Call numbers (LC, Dewey, PRONTO): how to find books by call number.
   4. Cover MIRLYN subject and keyword searching. Mention the "sm" search.

   Teaching Method: Lecture demonstration with everyone expected to conduct at least one search in each system.
   Application: Access exercise and some desk work.

D. Articles (unknown items): use indexes which will be covered in other sessions.Simply mention this as part of the logical progression here. Show Wilson Databases (DWIL), Public Affairs Information Service (PAIS), and Psychology Abstracts (PSYC) on MIRLYN; search techniques the same as used with Michigan Online Catalog (MCAT).

E.   Wrap-up: Give them Access Exercise. It's due in one week to their
     supervisor.

Assignment: Have them complete exercise before next training session.
                      Have them practice MIRLYN searches on their own.
Desk Work: Have them continue observation. Begin to handle
                      directional and simple questions as soon as they feel
                      ready.
Handouts: MIRLYN Quick Guide brochure and keyword/boolean
                      handout; 2 readings on questioning technique (to be
                      discussed in session IV); Access Exercise.

SESSION IV

Reference Interview and Search Strategy

A.   Brief review of reference philosophy
     · Concept of teaching library and UGL's role
     Concept of active reference
     Concept of creating and maintaining good patron relations
     Give assignment to them.

     Teaching Method: Discussion. Encourage people to share
     examples of the philosophy in action or being violated, different
     philosophies they might know of or expect. If they are unable to do
     so, provide concrete examples on each point. (This is a good
     opportunity to reinforce the ground rule that all class discussions are
     confidential and are not to contain clues as to the identities of any
     individuals or libraries.)
     Application: Have them do the homework for this topic in which
     they write down two things they taught, two examples of their efforts
     to practice proactive reference, and two things they do to create or
     maintain good patron relations. They are to hand that brief list in to
     their supervisor in a week. It will be returned to them shortly with
     brief comments and/or suggestions.

B.   Reference interview
     What it is; why do it; how to do it {using tact, non-intrusive
     questions}. Discuss neutral questions and general techniques as
     discussed in last session's reading assignment.
     As time permits, observe and participate in skits by reference staff.
     Discuss skits. Skits vary but each is intended to present a realistic
     situation and illustrate a basic principle of the reference interview
     process. Sample situations include dealing with a problem patron and
     working with a patron carefully enough to discover that a request for
     books on Florida actually means a request for pictures of palm trees.
     (When staff is too busy to have skits, have students go through mock
     questioning sessions using recent desk questions.) Distribute
     Observation Forms and encourage them to start a little self-observation.

Discuss referrals and Term Paper Assistance Program (TAP). When they are appropriate and how to do them. Give them a copy of the TAP form.

Teaching Method: Skits, lecture, discussion.
Application: Have them use the observation form for a little self-observation. Encourage them to hand it in to their supervisor for comments and feedback.

C. Search strategy
    What it is; how to do it; standard 4-step strategy; question analysis. Distribute copies of strategy and question analysis guide.

    Teaching Method: Exercise and discussion. As a group, they generate a search strategy for at least one question. Encourage people to share examples of search strategies they might know of or expect. If they are unable to do so, provide concrete examples on each point.
    Application: Have them write down everything they did on two of the more complex questions they answered while at the reference desk. (This part of the homework sheet mentioned above.)

Assignment: Read chapter five from THE REFERENCE INTERVIEW AS A CREATIVE ART by the Jennerichs and "Search Strategy in the Research Process" from Beaubian, Hogan, and George, LEARNING THE LIBRARY.
Desk Work: Continue observation. Begin to handle reference questions as they feel ready. Hand in the homework assignment plus, if they feel ready, the observation form.
Handouts: Copies of two readings; Research Strategy; Question Analysis; Observation Form; Reference Interview Exercise; TAP form.

SESSION V

Basic Reference Tools

A. Discussion of readings assigned from last week.
B. Fact tools: Move through reference stacks and highlight the most commonly used tools in each subject area. Point out only one or two per field. This is to give an overview of the type of material most often requested, not to introduce them to every title. Point out the aspects to look for in a tool: arrangement, access, type of information, level of detail given, scope, currency. Use the time to reinforce an understanding of the basic LC subject divisions. Distribute copies of Basic Reference Sources.

    Teaching Method: Lecture, demonstration with discussion and questions.
    Application: Exercise

C. Finding tools: Move through reference stacks and highlight the most commonly used tools in each subject area. Point out the arrangement of the index tables. This is to give an overview of the type of material most often requested, not to introduce them to every title. Point out the aspects to look for in a tool: arrangement, access, type of information, level of detail given, scope, electronic counterparts, currency. Use the time to reinforce an understanding of the basic LC subject divisions, if that seems appropriate given the needs of the group.

D. Wrap-up: Give them Reference Runaround Exercise and set a due date. Discuss the fact that UGL does not have some alternative press indexes and tools. Remind them of referral policy.

Teaching Method: Lecture, demonstration with discussion and questions.
Application: Exercise

Assignment:	Give them the Reference Runaround Exercise and the Periodical Index Exercise. Have them answer every question and discuss the answers with any full-time reference staff member or their supervisor. The results are to be handed in to their supervisor within one week.
Desk Work:	Begin to move more into answering some reference questions.
Handouts:	Reference Runaround Exercise; Basic Reference Sources; list of UGL periodical indexes; Periodical Index Exercise.

SESSION VI

Automated Services

A. Overview of UGL automated services
   a. Online search services: procedures and policies. Essentially, these people refer all such requests unless they receive special additional training from the Coordinator for Automated Services.
   b. Review MIRLYN, RLIN
   c. Mention Microcomputer Center, UM Medline, and MTS

   Teaching Method: Lecture, demonstration with discussion and questions.
   Application: Online Exercise

B. How to handle all end-user services: instruction, demo, repairs, supplies
   a. InfoTrac
   b. Readers' Guide
   c. National Newspaper Index
   d. Reader/printer

Teaching Method: Lecture, demonstration with discussion and questions.
Application: CD ROM Exercise

Assignment:	Give them exercises. Have them answer every question and discuss the answers with any full-time reference staff member or their supervisor. The results are to be handed in to their supervisor within one week.
Desk Work:	Encourage them to observe and work at MIRLYN workstations as well as their regular work at the reference desk.
Handouts:	Copies of UGL handouts for CD ROM products; Staff Mode handouts for MIRLYN; Online Exercise; CD ROM Exercise.

FURTHER TRAINING:

During the ensuing semester, hold a series of sessions to review tools by subject.   The subjects covered might include such areas as the following: biographical, literary criticism, statistics, political science, science, education, business.   For each section, cover the following: fact tools, finding tools, most commonly asked questions, proper referrals, and search strategy. Sessions could last from 30 to 50 minutes. On certain days it might work out best to schedule a few topics together.

Teaching Method: Lecture, demonstration with discussion and questions.
Application: Have them keep a running list of the titles they have used, leave questions in the reference log about sources they needed but couldn't find or sources they enjoyed using. Tell them to make log entries on at least two titles or questions per subject covered.

Desk Work: Continue handling questions.

IV. HANDOUTS FOR TRAINEES

Session I
* First timecard
* Student Employee Handbook
* Training outline and schedule
* Guide to Graduate Library
* Self-guided tour
* Basic Information Form

Session II
* UGL Reference Area Checklist
* Opening and Closing the Reference Desk
* Self-guided tour
* Emergency procedures
* Commonly Asked Questions

Session III
* MIRLYN brochure and keyword/boolean handout
* Access Exercise
* Two readings on questioning

Session IV
* Research Strategy
* Question Analysis
* Observation form
* Reference Interview Exercise
* TAP Form

Session V
* Reference Runaround Exercise
* Periodical Index Exercise
* Basic Reference Sources
* List of UGL periodical indexes

Session VI
* Copies of UGL handouts for CD ROM products
* Staff Mode handouts for MIRLYN
* Online Exercise
* CD ROM Exercise

V. TRAINING AIDS FOR INSTRUCTORS AND TRAINEES

UGL REFERENCE AREA CHECKLIST FOR NEW REFERENCE STAFF MEMBERS

Desk #1
-Reference log and clipboard
  -Recording statistics
  -Schedule sheets
  -General contents
  -Emergency procedures
-Keys: file, bins, Academic
    Resource Center, etc.
-Sign-out slips
-Supplies: pencils, scissors, etc.

Desk #2
-Statistics sheets
-PIC office key

Reference Desk Filing Cabinet
-Rolodex
-Policies and Procedures Manual
-Telephone and answering machine
-Forms (MIRLYN errors, pages
    missing, TAP, etc.)
-General contents
-Pamphlet file (bottom drawer)

Bin #1
-Contents
-Check out rules and procedures

Bin #2
-Contents and their use

Microform Collections
-College catalogs and their indices
-Phonefiche and their guide
-Refiling; other fiche
-Microfilm collection
-Microform readers and the
    reader/printer with its supplies

Periodicals
-Location of bound/unbound
-Location of other serial lists

Serials/Acquisitions Office
-Problem serials
-Michigan Daily, University Record
-Backup supplies for computers

Catalog
-Handicap access to MIRLYN
    & LCSH
-Special catalogs such as plays
-LCSH

Reserves
-Play collection catalog
-Masterplots catalog and notebook
-Cassette collection catalog
-Copy machines and
    MIRLYN stations

Computers
-What's what
  --Paper under bins and in closet
  --Ribbons and ink
-Care and feeding
  --Paperclip trick
  --Fixing paper/ink problems
  --(Re)starting
  --Phone numbers for problems
  --Repair procedures
  --Changing CDs

Reference Collection
-Index locations
  --Index shelves,
    reference shelves
  --Index tables
-Annual reviews
-New book shelves
-Reshelving counter

OPENING AND CLOSING THE REFERENCE DESK

It is important that the Reference Desk be opened promptly. If an emergency arises which will keep you from arriving on time or force you to leave early, you *must* contact your supervisor (Reference Coordinator, PIC Coordinator, Student Assistant Supervisor) or another member of the reference department as soon as possible so that s/he may plan for uncovered hours.

If patrons are waiting with questions when you arrive at the desk, of course you should go ahead and answer their questions while starting to open the desk. If the question will take you away from the desk for an extended time, at least set up the telephone. If they are waiting when it is time to close the desk, go ahead and begin the closing procedures. You may wish to inform those waiting that the desk is closing and you can take only short questions (or one more question, etc.). It may be possible to refer patrons to other information services (e.g. Graduate Library Information Desk) if those service points are still open.

Because of the many demands on staff time, it is our policy not to open the desk early or to close it late. Staff must be very consistent in acting on this policy so that all patrons receive the same level of service. Staff should not feel they must open prior to the scheduled time or close after posted hours despite patron demands. Patrons may be referred to other information services; complaints should be referred to the Coordinator for Reference and BI.

Opening Procedures

1. Retrieve the reference desk key from the mailbox at the circulation desk.
2. Unlock reference desk 1 where you will find the keys to the filing cabinet under the reference desk.
3. Put on your name tag.
4. Unlock the filing cabinet. Remove the telephone and plug it in. Change the answering machine tape and set switch to delay.
5. Boot the reference desk MIRLYN terminal. Remove the PC-Tie disk.
6. Check all computer workstations to make sure they are working properly, have working printers, and are relatively neat.
7. Boot the terminal on the right with Smartcom: hit [return twice for day and time] and type "scom" and [return].
8. Put new statistics sheets in both slots. Date each sheet.
9. Check the reference log for new information. Be sure to record any problems encountered.
10. Put out supplies for patrons such as pencils, scratch paper, stapler and tape.
11. Tidy the reference area if necessary.

Closing Procedures
1. Lock the bins. If any bin materials are checked out, give the charge slips to circulation.
2. Unplug the telephone at the phone end and put both the phone and the tip of the cord in the filing cabinet. Change the tape in the answering machine and set the response switch to immediate.
3. Turn off Smartcom and return the disk to the file. Anything that has been taken from the filing cabinet (e.g. phone books, tape, stapler, etc.) should be replaced. Replace the log in the top drawer of filing cabinet and lock it.
4. Clear off the reference desk and lock both drawers.
5. Logoff MIRLYN.
6. Return the key to the circulation desk.

CHECKLIST FOR UGL TOUR

In each area, explain how the reference desk relates to the questions involving it. Explain basic procedures. Try to be aware of the unspoken assumptions about who may walk where and do what in each area. Think about things from the viewpoint of personal use.

BASEMENT:

Copiers
Stacks office
Copy card machine
Water fountains
Elevators
Shelflist
Calling for copier repairs at all times

Change machines
Visit stacks personnel
Restrooms
Books on top of stacks
Classroom for videos and BI
Money lost in machines

FIRST FLOOR:

Circulation
searches
explain their own rules
help when MIRLYN's down
no change
not for reserve books
keeps handicap door clear

bar codes
lost & found
reference mailboxes
Security calls in emergency
free campus phone

Reference
desk
staff only MIRLYN station

bin area is not for public use
handicap table for LCSH & MIRLYN

Acquisitions
repairs room
DAILY
computer supply backups
damaged volumes: give Kevin books; give Julie serials (missing page reports)

periodicals
RECORD

Staff Lounge
refrigerator - cleaned out on Fridays   microwave, few dishes

SECOND FLOOR:

Academic Resource Center   Systems Office
study room   Film and Video Library

THIRD FLOOR:

Reserve desk   Coin copy machine
MIRLYN   Reserve Office
Engineering/Transportation Library
Staff copier (must get card from staff member to use it)

FOURTH FLOOR:

Microcomputer Center   Low vision room
CAEN Lab   Staff elevator
Engineering/Transportation Library

GENERAL:

coin and card machines   water fountain
closet with paper   restrooms
pencil sharpener   wall maps
student lounge & papers   elevators
stairs   emergency exits
fire alarms   offices
first aid kit in Marjorie's office   PIC office
classroom for videos and BI   money lost in machines
phones   suggestion box
feedback board
supply cabinet (need to have staff member get things for them)

Where they put personal belongings while working (e.g. an office rather than behind the desk if at all possible, at least out of public sight at the desk)

NO food/drink/smoking in building except for consumables in lounges

UGL EVACUATION PLAN

Possible situations for the implementation of the evacuation plan: fire, a sighted bomb, tornado (evacuate to the basement), or whenever we are told to by Security.

General Information

1. Try to remain calm. If you panic, the patrons will panic.
2. Close doors behind you if you are the last to leave a room.
3. IF YOU CAN'T CONTACT THE NEXT PERSON OR AREA ON THE PLAN, YOU MUST CARRY OUT THEIR DUTIES.
4. If you call 911 (Security), be sure to tell the UGL Circulation Desk and pull the nearest fire alarm.
5. One person on each floor needs to be responsible for making sure the floor is entirely empty before they leave. This will be done on a volunteer basis. Please don't volunteer if you don't feel you can stay in the building the extra time in an evacuation situation.
6. If you are away from your normal work area do not try to get back to your area. You automatically become part of the evacuation for that area or floor. Go to the contact point for the floor you are on and ask what you can do to help. The contact points are as follows:

Fourth Floor	Microcomputer Center Desk
Third Floor	Engineering/Trans. Circulation Desk
Second Floor	Film and Video Library
First Floor	Circulation Desk
Basement	Stacks Office

7. If someone won't leave after you have told them to evacuate, get a witness and tell them to leave again. If they still won't leave, tell Security or Circulation on your way out of the building.
8. Handicapped persons requiring assistance evacuation will have been instructed by the P.A. announcement to wait near the "staircase located toward the front of the building." If you see someone there, be sure to tell Circulation so that they can alert Security.
9. Someone on each floor will have to flick the lights on and off to alert the Hearing-Impaired patrons to the emergency.
10. USE YOUR COMMON SENSE IN ALL SITUATIONS.

EVACUATION PLAN FOR THE REFERENCE DESK

PERSON # 1

CALL ACQUISITIONS FIRST: 4-4410

If you get no answer, call the following numbers
in succession until you find someone:

1.	Room 125	4-4426
2.	Room 124	4-4481
3.	Room 123	4-4449
4.	Room 122	4-4479
5.	Room 121	3-9761

PERSON # 2

Help evacuate patrons from the main study areas
including the back to the exits.
Check PIC office and Room 120. Flick lights on and off to alert
Hearing-Impaired patrons. The switch is by the front door.

CLOSE DOORS WHEN LEAVING AN AREA.

**REPORT HANDICAPPED PERSONS NEEDING ASSISTANCE
TO THE CIRCULATION STAFF.**

EVACUATION PLAN FOR THE REFERENCE DESK
ONE PERSON ON THE DESK

---

1. Evacuate Microfilm Area

2. Evacuate PIC room (114)

3. Evacuate Back Study Area

4. Evacuate Classroom (120)

5. Evacuate all offices (121-126)

Flick lights on and off to alert Hearing-Impaired patrons.
The switch is by the front door.

CLOSE DOORS WHEN LEAVING AN AREA.

EVACUATE ALL STUDY AREAS.

**REPORT HANDICAPPED PERSONS NEEDING ASSISTANCE
TO THE CIRCULATION STAFF.**

COMMONLY ASKED QUESTIONS

Below are a few of the most frequently asked questions pertaining to locations in and use of the Undergraduate Library. The information given in response to each question is not necessarily sufficient to meet a patron's needs completely, but it represents the absolute minimum you should know about the library before you become at all active during your observation periods. Until you acquire a more complete knowledge of the UGL you will be expected to be able to provide at least initial help to library users who have these questions.

1. **Where is the Reserve Desk? How do I get a book that's on reserve?**
   The desk (now referred to as the University Library Reserve Service) is on the third floor opposite the elevators. Materials for both graduate and undergraduate courses are on reserve here. There are notebooks on shelves opposite the desk which list by department, course number, and name of instructor all books and periodical articles on reserve for various courses. Call numbers for both books and periodical articles are given next to each title. Periodical articles for a given course are found on a separate page immediately following the book list for the same course. To obtain an item from Reserve, the requestor should write its call number on one of the call slips found on the tables near the desk and drop the call slip in the box on the desk. When an item has been located by Reserve Service attendants and is ready to check out, the requestor's name will be called. A current U-M ID card is needed to check out Reserve material.

2. **Can I borrow a pen or pencil?**
   We do not loan pens to patrons but we do provide "golf" pencils in reference desk #1. Just set some out on the desk and let people take what they need.

3. **Where's the pencil sharpener?**
   Located next to the large Ann Arbor map on the wall by the card catalog.

4. **How can I find a book? Where can I check out a book?**
   The MCAT portion of MIRLYN lists books by author, title, and subject. Ask for help at the reference desk to locate a particular book. If you have already found the MCAT entry for a book, locate the call number which is on the MCAT screen under "call number". If a MCAT record shows that UGL does not own the book in question then you must go to the owning library to get it. The location chart on the far wall tells you which floor a UGL book will be shelved on, according to the first letter of its call number. Books are arranged on the shelves alphabetically according to the first line, then numerically by the second line, and so on. Library users can go to the shelves, get their own books and take them with their ID cards to the circulation desk in the lobby to be checked out. There's no limit on the number of books which can be taken out. Generally speaking, reference books and periodicals do not circulate.

5. **Where are the periodicals?**
   In general, the most recent issues are kept at the Reserve Desk on the third floor. Bound volumes, usually from the previous thirty years, are shelved at the back of the main floor, in the area to the left of the main

aisle under the sign "Bound Periodicals". They are in alphabetical order by title.

6. **Where are the copy machines?**
There are several copiers in the basement, two at the back of the first floor to the left of the periodicals, and one in the Reserve room on the third floor. Copies cost ten cents a page or seven cents a page with a copy card. A coin operated machine is in the Reserve room, on the main floor near the periodicals and in the basement. Copy card vending machines are located in the basement as are change machines. Report all refund and machine complaints directly to Circulation. If the problem is bad enough to disrupt service (such as several machines out or the coin operated machines out) then tell circulation to call for emergency repairs even during night and weekend hours.

7. **Do you have any change?**
No service point in the library gives out change, including the reference desk. There is a dollar bill changer in the basement near the copiers. In addition, the vending machines in the student lounge give change if you buy something. Report all refund and machine complaints directly to Circulation.

8. **Do you have a map of Ann Arbor?**
Yes, a large one on the front wall of the main floor reading room, to the left as you face the lobby. Also notice the Michigan map on the wall at right angles to the Ann Arbor map. There is also a fold-out map of Ann Arbor in the pamphlet file which is located in the bottom drawer of the reference desk file cabinet.

9. **Can I use your telephone? or Is there a telephone here I can use?**
Patrons can not use the reference desk phone. There is a pay phone in the corridor behind the stairwell on the main floor (opposite the rest rooms). From the reference desk, go through the door next to the microfilm readers. All the other floors have pay phones as well. There is a free campus phone near the circulation desk.

10. **Where are the rest rooms and drinking fountains?**
Both are located in the same corridor as the telephone. Phones, fountains, and rest rooms are in the same location on all floors of the building except the fourth.

11. **Do you have phone books from other cities?**
We have phone fiche for the state of Michigan and other selected cities around the country. The fiche and notebook to explain how to use the fiche are located on the long reference shelf underneath the bins. Encourage patrons who use this set to put their fiche in the refiling box when they are finished. The Graduate Library has the entire Phonefiche of the United States which includes most U.S. phone books and some foreign countries. An Ann Arbor phone book as well as the student and staff directories is kept in the reference file cabinet.

12. **I can't find my class! Where's the C.C. Little Building? or What does CCL mean? That's where my class meets.**
We keep a current UM time schedule in bin 1 and it will usually decode the building abbreviations for you. You can also give these people a copy of the university map from the stack on the table next to the desk.

13. **Where are the college catalogs?**
Catalogs for most of the UM schools and colleges are kept in bin 1. A microfiche collection of catalogs from universities across the country is available on the long reference shelf underneath the bins. Encourage patrons who use this set to put their fiche in the refiling box when they are finished. The Graduate Library has the entire United States and some foreign countries on fiche.

14. **Where can I listen to tapes or watch a video?**
The Sight and Sound Center used to be the answer to this question but it closed in 1984. Videos, mainly Shakespeare plays, are scheduled for class showings in room 120 or room 24 by the Film and Video Library. A listing of those showings is in the "Important Information" section of the reference notebook. Another possible resource is the Film and Video Library itself which has an office on the second floor of the UGL. Language tapes and so on are not available at UGL. Audio cassette recordings that are still found in the small card catalog occasionally can be obtained at the Reserve Desk. For all audio materials, see the Policies and Procedures Manual.

15. **Do you get any newspapers here? Where are they?**
The only newspaper we keep on microfilm is the *New York Times*. We keep one year's worth of the *Michigan Daily* and the *Record* in the Acquisitions Office, room 126. Other than that, we do receive and put out each day in the student lounge a wide selection of national and Michigan newspapers. We only keep the most recent editions of these papers; for back issues of most of these papers and for other titles, refer patrons to the Graduate Library's Serial Services.

16. **Where's the Engineering/Transportation Library?**
It's a completely separate library located on the third floor and part of the fourth floor of the UGL building. It has its own reference service. Be aware that many people associated with the Engineering School, faculty and students alike, say "Ugli" when they mean "Engineering Library". If a library user complains of being unable to find material that the "prof said was here", the problem could be that s/he's in the wrong library. A fair number of people outside the University community come to our reference desk looking for patents and should be sent directly upstairs; occasionally when the Engineering reference desk is not staffed these people will try to get assistance from the UGL desk. We don't *do* patents.

17. **Where is the math tutoring?**
An Engineering Fraternity has math tutors available in the Engineering Library during much of Fall and Winter terms.

18. **What time is it?**
There is a clock in the middle of the front wall of the main floor, above the reference stacks.

19. **Where are the smoking areas?**
Just outside the front doors!

20. **Can I borrow a calculator?**
There are three available for public use in the Engineering Library on the third floor. Library users should inquire about them at the Engineering Library circulation desk.

21. **Where can I find a book with a 999 call number? or Where is PRONTO?**
   The PRONTO collection is a rotating collection of current fiction and non-fiction, shelved in the browsing area in the lobby and available for three-week circulation. These books have Dewey or Dewey-like call numbers (such as 999) to distinguish them from the rest of the collection.

22. **Where can I do my word processing?**
   The Microcomputer Center on the fourth floor of the UGL has over 70 Zenith and Macintosh stations. MIRLYN can be accessed on the Zeniths and word processing can be done up there. The laser printer is available to all who can use the Center. A current UM ID card is required to use the Center. PIC staff will teach anyone how to do word processing in the ARC.

RESEARCH STRATEGY

There are many different research strategies. The one outlined below is the most basic and one of the most commonly used. With each reference interview, try to get a firm grasp of at least two points:

   (1)   What disciplines or fields of study are involved? Material in the hard sciences will come out first in journals while material relating to current events can come out first in newspapers and reference tools such as the *Congressional Quarterly Almanac*.

   (2)   How far has the patron gotten in the strategy? People will ask for material in step four when they really need step one. Sometimes they're right of course, but do think about what they need rather than what they say they need.

I.   Research strategy
   A.   **Define and focus topic**
      1.   Use annual reviews and subject encyclopedias to get ideas.
      2.   Use a relevant periodical index to get idea of how much material is available on the topic.
   B.   **Gather background** on topic; get context; understand major ideas; find experts
      1.   Specialized dictionaries provide expert definitions in depth.
      2.   Specialized encyclopedias often provide an easy overview with a bibliography of key works at the end of the article.
      3.   Remember that many topics are interdisciplinary so works in law, medicine, education, social work, feminism, and so on may be of use as well.
   C.   **Gather older material**, i.e. books
      1.   Explain basic idea of LCSH.
      2.   Point out that MIRLYN is the only place on campus to find records of new books and that much of the conversion process has been completed.
      3.   Refer them to the two main handouts on MIRLYN.

4. Remind them to try the card catalog in the Graduate Library if they can not find what they need in MIRLYN and to ask at a reference desk if they are still not satisfied.
D. **Gather newest material,** i.e. journal, magazine, and newspaper articles
   1. Cover the difference between magazine and journal articles; emphasize the difference between popular and scholarly literature.
   2. Explain the mechanics of the relevant periodical indexes.
   3. Point out the value of using keyword access and boolean searching, when appropriate.
   4. Tell them how to find the periodicals once they have the citations. Point out that MIRLYN is usually the fastest way to go; how our journals are arranged; that they are more than welcome in any of the libraries which house their journals.

QUESTION ANALYSIS

When you provide information for a patron, consider the following questions. They may give you a new viewpoint or a deeper understanding of the information need. Consider asking the patron to think about some of the questions.

Do any words require definition?
What are the subquestions involved?
What time frames are involved?
What disciplines are involved?
What formats will you expect to find?
What will you need to support your argument?
How much information do you need to find?

BASIC REFERENCE SOURCES

The titles listed below represent UGL's more commonly used reference books. Please familiarize yourself with each of them, then move on to learning the rest of the collection. Remember to check the new reference book shelves regularly. As always, if you have any questions, just ask.

Africa South of the Sahara	DT 352 .A1 A24
Almanac of American Politics	JK 1012 .A44
Book Review Index	Z 1035. A1 B72
Contemporary Literary Criticism	PN 41 .C76
Current Biography	CT 100 .C98
Dictionary of Literary Biography	PS 21 .D55
Encyclopedia of Associations	AS 22. E56
Europa Yearbook	D 2 .E92
Familiar Quotations	PN 6081 .B289
Far East and Australasia	DS 502 .F22

Grove Dictionary of Music and Musicians	ML 100 .N53
Guide to American Law	KF 156 .G771
Handbook of Chemistry and Physics (CRC Handbook)	QD 65 .C517h
Information Please Almanac	AY 64 .I43
International Encyclopedia of the Social Sciences	H 41 .I58
McGraw Hill Encyclopedia of Science and Technology	Q 121 .M15 1982
Middle East and North Africa	DS 49 .M63
Oxford English Dictionary	PE 1625 .M982
Peterson's Graduate Programs	LB 2371 .A59
Peterson's Guide to Four Year Colleges	L 901 .A621
Standard and Poor's Register	HG 4057 .A2 P82
Statistical Abstract of the United States	HA 202
United States Government Manual	JK 421 .A3
World Book Encyclopedia	AE 5 .W551

SIGNON TO MIRLYN IN STAFF MODE

- Put PC-Tie in Drive A
- Turn on computer and monitor
- At the ">", press [RETURN]
- At the "Which host?" prompt type [PASSWORD] and press [RETURN] or type [F1]
- At "Welcome to UM Libraries..." type [PASSWORD] and press [RETURN]
- At "Welcome to the MIRLYN Production System..." type [Ctrl] [F2]
- On blank screen, type [PASSWORD] and press [RETURN]
- After *userid* type "ctrl u" and [PASSWORD]; ta_b to *password* and type "ctrl u" and [PASSWORD]. Press [RETURN] (ctrl u clears the field, which appears to be clear but is not. Don't ask.)
- On blank screen type "ltul" or "lnav"

To transfer from Staff Mode to Public Catalog
- Type [Ctrl] [F2] until screen is blank
- Type "lnav"

SIGNON AND SIGNOFF INSTRUCTIONS

Signon to MIRLYN Public Catalog
- Put PC-Tie in Drive A
- Turn on computer and monitor
- At the ">", press [RETURN]
- At the "Which host?" prompt type "mirlyn" and press [RETURN]
- At "Welcome to the UM Libraries..." press [RETURN]

Signon to MIRLYN in **Staff Mode**
- Put PC-Tie in Drive A
- Turn on computer and monitor
- At the ">", press [RETURN]
- At the "Which host?" prompt type [PASSWORD] and press [RETURN] or type [F1]
- At "Welcome to UM Libraries..." type [PASSWORD] and press [RETURN]
- At "Welcome to the MIRLYN Production System..." type [Ctrl] [F2]
- On blank screen, type [PASSWORD] and press [RETURN]
- After userid type "control U" and [PASSWORD]; tab to password and type "control U" and [PASSWORD]. Press [RETURN]
- On blank screen type [PASSWORD] or [PASSWORD]
To transfer from Staff Mode to Public Catalog
  - Type [Ctrl] [F2] until screen is blank
  - Type [PASSWORD]
To transfer from Public Catalog to Staff Mode when signed onto MIRLYN-staff
  - Type [Ctrl] [F2] until screen is blank
  - Type [PASSWORD]
To transfer from Public Catalog to Staff Mode when signed onto the Public Catalog
  - Type [Ctrl] [F3]
  - Type [Ctrl] [F9] or "%exit"
  - At "Which host?" type [PASSWORD] and [RETURN] and signon to staff mode as above
To **signoff** from MIRLYN Public Catalog
- Type [Ctrl] [F3]
- Type [Ctrl] [F9] or "%exit" to get to the "Which host?" prompt OR
- Type [Ctrl] [F10] to signoff MTS
To **signoff** from MIRLYN Staff Mode
- Type [Ctrl] [F2] until screen is blank
- Type cssf logoff
- Type [Ctrl] [F3]
- Type [Ctrl] [F9] or "%exit" to get to the "Which host?" prompt OR
- Type [Ctrl] [F10] to signoff MTS

STAFF MODE SEARCH COMMANDS

author searching	ltul fi ja=obrien james
	ltul fi ja=united states congress
title searching	ltul fi jt=whos who in america
subject searching	ltul fi js=crime and criminals -biography
	(space dash, not 2 dashes)
	ltul fi js=afro-american art

dictionary searching	ltul fi jx=haunts
keyword searching	not available
name authority	ltul fi fn=clemens samuel
call number	ltul fi cl=jk 1001 .c 75 or ltul fi cl=jk1001.c75 (fuzzy) ltul fi cd=350 944 a 21685 or ltul fi cd=350.944a21685 (fuzzy) ltul fi co=video
lccn number	ltul fi nl=85-13568
isbn number	ltul fi nb=0-06-055194-1 or ltul fi nb=0060551941
issn number	ltul fi ns=0362-076x or ltul fi ns=0362076x
rlin record number	ltul fi no=miug86-b2669
mirlyn record number	ltul fi acf6163

You can find private copies and other uncataloged material *on course reserve* (this does **not** include uncataloged permanent closed reserves such as the drama collection):

reserve book by author	ltul fi ra=
reserve book by title	ltul fi rt=
reserve books by professor	ltul fi ri=
reserve books by course name abbreviations)	ltul fi rc= (need to know course

VI. REFERENCE HELPERS FOR TRAINEES

MAJOR REFERENCE TOOLS, BY CALL NUMBER

GENERAL WORKS

Encyclopaedia Britannica	AE 5 .E56 1987
World Book	AE 5 .W551 1988
World of Learning	AS 2 .W93
Acronyms, Initialisms, and Abbreviations Dictionary	AS 8 .A187
Encyclopedia of Associations	AS 22 .E56
World Almanac	AY 67 .N5W9
Ann Arbor City Directory	AY 2001 .A39

PHILOSOPHY, PSYCHOLOGY, RELIGION

World Philosophy	B 29 .W681 1982
Dictionary of the History of Ideas	B 51 .D55
Encyclopedia of Philosophy	B 51 .E56
Encyclopedia of Psychology	BF 31 .E521 1984
Personality Tests and Reviews	BF 698.5 .B97
Encyclopedia of Religion	BL 31 .E461 1987
Encyclopedia of Religion and Ethics	BL 31 .E8
World Christian Encyclopedia	BR 95 .W93
Analytical Concordance to the Bible	BS 425 .Y75 1955
Bibles	BS
New Catholic Encyclopedia	BX 841 .N55

HISTORY (GENERAL)

Current Biography	CT 100 .C98
Encyclopedia of World Biography	CT 103 .M15
Dictionary of American Biography	CT 213 .D55

HISTORY AND TOPOGRAPHY (GENERALLY EXCLUDING AMERICA)

Europa Yearbook	D 2 .E92
Chronology of World History	D 11 .F86 1975
Almanac of Dates	D 11.5 .M5651
Chase's Annual Events	D 11.5 .C49
Great Events from History	D 59 .M261
Facts on File	D 410 .F14
Keesing's Contemporary Archives	D 410 .K263
Historical Encyclopedia of World War II	D 740 .E553
New Century Classical Handbook	DE 5 .N53
USSR Facts and Figures Annual	DK 1 .U13
Middle East and North Africa	DS 49 .M63
Encyclopedia Judaica	DS 102.8 .E53
Far East and Australasia	DS 502 .F22
China Facts and Figures Annual	DS 779.15 .C48
Africa South of the Sahara	DT 352 .A1 A24

HISTORY--AMERICA--GENERAL
State Names, Seals, Flags, and Symbols	E 155 .S441 1987
Worldmark Encyclopedia of the States	E156 .W671
Dictionary of American History	E 174 .D55 1976
Chronology of the United States	E 174.5 .C631
Who's Who in American Politics	E 840.6 .W63
Great Events from History: American Series	E 178 .M221
Harvard Encyclopedia of American Ethnic Groups	E 184 .A1 H351
Negro Almanac	E 185 .P73 1983

History--America--Local
Washington Information Directory	F 192.5 .W324

GEOGRAPHY, ANTHROPOLOGY
Webster's New Geographical Dictionary	G 103.5 .W38 1984
New State of the World Atlas	G 1021 .K461 1987b
Atlases	G 102 and following
Mythical and Fabulous Creatures	GR 825 .M871 1987
Scarne's Encyclopedia of Games	GV 1229 .S29

SOCIAL SCIENCES
Dictionary of the Social Sciences	H 41 .G72
International Encyclopedia of the Social Sciences	H 41 .I58
Statistical Yearbook	HA 40 .C8 U53
Statistical Abstract of the US	HA 202
Historical Statistics of the US	HA 202 .A2
New Book of American Rankings	HA 214 .N491
Michigan Statistical Abstract	HA 441 .M62
Demographic Yearbook	HB 881 .A2 U5
Broadcasting and Cablecasting Yearbook	HE 8700.7 .C6 B87
Standard and Poor's Register	HG 4057 .A2 P82
Encyclopedia of Feminism	HQ 1115 .T871 1986
Encyclopedia of Crime and Justice	HV 6017 .E521 1983

POLITICAL SCIENCE
International Yearbook and Statemen's Who's Who	JA 51.I6
Constitutions of Nations	JF 11 .P36
Congressional Quarterly	JK 1 .C12
Congressional Quarterly Almanac	JK 1 .C756
US Government Manual	JK 421 .A3
Politics of America	JK 1010 .P76
PAC Directory	JK 1991 .P111
Michigan Manual	JK 5831

LAW
Black's Law Dictionary	KF 156 .B531
Guide to American Law	KF 156 G771
Encyclopedia of the American Constitution	KF 4548 .E531

EDUCATION

International Handbook of Universities	L 900 .I58
Peterson's Guide to 4 Year Colleges	L 901 .A621
American Universities and Colleges	LA 226 .A72
Directory of American Scholars	LA 2311 .D62
Financial Aids	LB 2338 .F47
International Encyclopedia of Education	LB 15 .I569
International Encyclopedia of Higher Education	LB 15 .I571
Mental Measurements Yearbook	LB 1131 .A1R97
See also Tests in Print	Z 5814 .E9
Personality Tests and Reviews	BF 698.5 .B97
Commonwealth Universities Yearbook	LB 2310 .C73
National Faculty Directory	LB 2331 .N277
Directory of Financial Aids for Minorities	LB 2338 .D561
Manual for Writers of Term Papers (Turabian)	LB 2369 .T93 1987
Peterson's Graduate Programs	LB 2371 .A59
History of the University of Michigan	LD 3278 .H665

MUSIC

Grove Dictionary of Music and Musicians	ML 100 .N53
New Oxford Companion to Music	ML 100 .N55
Baker's Biographical Dictionary of Musicians	ML 105 .B17 1984

FINE ARTS

Encyclopedia of World Art	N 31 .E543
Index to Artistic Biography	N 40 .H39
World Painting Index	ND 45 .H381

LANGUAGE

Foreign language dictionaries	PA-PL
Greek	PA 445
Latin	PA 2365
Italian	PC 1640
French	PC 2640
Spanish	PC 4640
Anglo-Saxon	PE 279
Middle English	PE 675
German	PF 3640
Russian	PG 2640
Hebrew	PJ 4833 .A34
Japanese	PL 679
Chinese	PL 1455 .M43
MLA Handbook for Writers of Research Papers	PE 478 .G43
Thesauruses	PE 1591
English language dictionaries	PE 1625-1628
Oxford English Dictionary (OED)	PE 1625 .M98

LITERATURE, THEATRE, TELEVISION, FILM

Cassell's Encyclopedia of World Literature	PN 41 .C34
Contemporary Literary Criticism	PN 41 .C76
Encyclopedia of World Literature in the 20th Century	PN 41 .L683
Literary terms and characters in general	PN 41-44
Literary Criticism from 1400-1800	PN 86 .L531
19th Century Literary Criticism	PN 92 N55
20th Century Literary Criticism	PN 94 .T94
Writer's Market	PN 161 .W96
Where Credit is Due	PN 171 .F56 S351
20th Century Authors and Supplements	PN 451 .K96
World Authors	PN 451 .W93
Princeton Handbook of Poetic Terms	PN 1042 .P751 1986
Critical Survey of Poetry: Foreign Language Series	PN 1111 .C711
Magill's Cinema Annual	PN 1993.3 .M19
Magill's American Film Guide	PN 1997.8 .M241
Critical Survey of Short Fiction	PN 3321 .C71
Science Fiction Reference Book	PN 3433.5 .S331
Critical Survey of Long Fiction: English Language Series	PN 3451 .C71
Critical Survey of Long Fiction: Foreign Language Series	PN 3451 .C992x
Granger's Index to Poetry	PN 4321 .G758
Quotation books	PN 6080-6426
British Writers	PR 85 .B86
Critical Survey of Poetry	PR 502 .C851
Critical Survey of Drama	PR 625 .C7411
Complete Concordance of Shakespeare	PR 2892 .B29
Shakespearean Criticism	PR 2965 .S43
Dictionary of Literary Biography	PS 21 .D55
American Writers	PS 129 .A513
See also Contemporary Authors	Z 1224 .C76

SCIENCE

McGraw-Hill Encyclopedia of Science and Technology	Q 121 .M15 1987
American Men and Women of Science	Q 141 .A49 1986
Handbook of Chemistry and Physics (CRC Handbook)	QD 65 .C517h
Lange's Handbook of Chemistry	QD 65 .L27b
Encyclopedia of Bioethics	QH 332 .E521
Grizmek's Animal Life Encyclopedia	QL 45.2 .G923

MEDICINE

Stedman's Medical Dictionary	R 121 .S812 1982
International Encyclopedia of Psychiatry, Psychology....	RC 334 .I5731
Diagnostic and Statistical Manual of Mental Disorders	RD 455.2 .C4 A515
Physician's Desk Reference	RS 75 .P57

TECHNOLOGY
McGraw-Hill Encyclopedia of Energy   TJ 163.2 .M15
World Encyclopedia of Food   TX 349 .C691

BIBLIOGRAPHY AND LIBRARY SCIENCE
Chicago Manual of Style   Z 253. C532
Book Review Index   Z 1053. A1 B72
Book Review Digest   Z 1219 .B722
Contemporary Authors   Z 1224 .C76
Indexes to ethnic American literature   Z 1229
Indexes to ethnic American studies   Z 1361
Poetry Explication   Z 2014 .P7 A73 1980
Chicorel Index to Plays, Poetry, Short Stories   Z 5781 .C53
Play Index   Z 5783 .P73
Film Review Index   Z 5784 .M9
Tests in Print   Z 5814 .E9 B98
Short Story Index   Z 5917 .S5 C77
20th-Century Short Story Explication   Z 5917 .S5 W18
Periodical Title Abbreviations   Z 6945 .A2 A44 1983
Complete Guide to Citing Government Documents   Z 7164 .G7 G371
Statistical Sources   Z 7551 .S79 1982

REFERENCE SOURCES: BY TITLE

Africa South of the Sahara   DT 352 .A1 A24
American Universities and Colleges   LA 226 .A72
Ann Arbor City Directory   AY 2001 .A39
Bartlett's Familiar Quotations   PN 6081 .B289
Book Review Digest   Z 1219 .B722
Book Review Index   Z 1035 .A1B72
CRC Handbook   QD 65 .C517h
Chicorel Theatre Index to Plays   Z 5781 .C53
City and County Data Book   HA 202 .A12
College Blue Book   LA 226 .H967
Complete Guide to Citing Government Documents   Z 7164 .G7 G371
Congress and the Nation   JK 1001 .C75
Congressional Quarterly Almanac   JK 1 .C756
Contemporary Authors   Z 1224 .C76
Current Biography   CT 100 .C98
Demographic Yearbook   HB 881 .A2 U5
Documents of American History   E 173. C73
Editor and Publisher Yearbook   Z 6941 .E22
Encyclopedia of Associations   AS 22 .E56
Encyclopedia of Bioethics   QH 332 .E521
Encyclopedia of Education   LB 15 .E55
Encyclopedia of Feminism   HQ 1115 .T871 1986
Encyclopedia of Philosophy   B 51 .E56
Encyclopedia of Social Work   HV 89 .S6

Encyclopedia of the Social Sciences	H 41 .E56
Encyclopedia of World Art	N 31 .E543
Ensian (the yearbook for UM)	LD 3297, open stacks
Europa Yearbook	D 2 .E92
Facts on File	D 410 .F14
Far East and Australasia	DS 502 .F22
Granger's Index to Poetry	PN 4321 .G75
Grove's Dictionary of Music and Musicians	ML 100 .G883
Handbook of Chemistry and Physics	QD 65 .C517h
Historical Statistics of the US	HA 202 .A2
International Encyclopedia of the Social Sciences	H 41 .I58
International Who's Who	CT 103 .I63
Literary Market Place	PN 161 .L78
Michigan Ensian (the yearbook for UM)	LD 3297, open stacks
Michigan Manual	JK 5831
Michigan Statistical Abstract	HA 441 .M62
Negro Almanac	E 185 .P73
OED (Oxford English Dictionary)	PE 1625 .M98
Ottemiller's Index to Plays in Collections	Z 5781 .O89
Oxford Companion to American Literature	PS 21 .H32
Oxford Companion to English Literature	PR 19 .H34
Oxford English Dictionary	PE 1625 .M98
Physician's Desk Reference	RS 75 .P57
Play Index	Z 5783 .P73
Poetry Explication	Z 2014 .P7 A73 1980
Robert's Rules of Order	JF 515 .R641
Science Fiction Reference Book	PN 3433.5. S331
Short Story Index	Z 5917 .S5 C77
Speech Index	AI 3 .S97
Statistical Abstract of the US	HA 202
Tests in Print	Z 5814 .E9
20th Century Authors	PN 771 .K96
20th-Century Short Story Explication	Z 5917 .S5 W18
Ulrich's International Periodicals Directory	Z 6941 .P461
United Nations Statistical Yearbook	HC 58 .U58
US Government Manual	JK 421 .A3
Where Credit is Due	PN 171 .F56 S351
Whitaker's Almanac	AY 754 .W6
Who's Who (British)	CT 770 .W6
Who's Who in America	CT 210 .W63
Who Was Who in America	CT 210 .W641
World Almanac	AY 67 .N5 W9

REFERENCE SOURCES: BY SUBJECT

African Americans
   Z 1361, E 185 .P73, L 901, PS 153, PN 6081.3 .Q671, NX 652, JK
   1924, PE 3727, N 6538
Almanacs
   AY 67 .N5 W9, AY 754 .W6, AY 414 .C1

American History
E 173 .C73, E 174
Animals
QL 5.2
Arabic world
DS 35, DS 49, DS 61-63
Art
N 31 .E543, N 6490 .O97, ND 45
Atlases
D 21.5 (historical), G 102 etc.
Biography
CT 100 .C98, CT 213 .D55, CT 773 .D47, CT 103 .I63, CT 210
.W641, CT 770 .W6, LB 2331 .N, PS 21 .D55
Book reviews
Z 1291, Z 1035
Business and economics
HB 61 .M15, HG 4057 .A2 P82
Chemistry
QD 65
Chronologies
D 9-21, E 174.5
Classics
DE 5 O98
Colleges
LA 226 .L78, L 901, L 900
Countries
DS 502 .F22, JA 51 .I6
Dictionaries
PE 1625 .M98 (OED), PE 1519 (rhyming), PE 1625-1628 (plain)

Greek	PA445	Latin	PA2365
Italian	PC1640	French	PC2640
Spanish	PC4640	Anglo-Saxon	PE279
Middle English	PE675	German	PF3640
Russian	PG2640	Hebrew	PJ4833.A34
Japanese	PL679	Chinese	PL1455.M43

Education
LB 15 .E55, LB 1131 .A
Etiquette
BJ 1853
Fashion
GT 510-737
Film
PN 1993.3, PN 1997.8, PN 1998.A
Financial Aid
LB 2337-8
Flags
CR 101-113
Folklore
GR 35, GR 67
Graduate Schools
LB 2371 .A59

Jewish Americans
   BM 50, BM 700, E 184 .J, Z 1361, DS 102.8 .E53
Latino Americans
   E 184 .M, Z 1361, PS 153 .M4
Law
   KF 156, KF 4548, HV 6017 .E521
Literature
   Z 1224. C76 & PN 771 .K96 (modern authors), Z 2011 .W34 (English
   bibliographies), PS 21 .H32 (American), PR 19 .H34 & PR 85
   (English), Z 1229 (ethnic), PS 21 .D55, PN 41 .C (world)
Medicine
   R 121, RS 356 .M, RS 75, QH 332 .E521
Minorities
   E 184, E 185, Z 1361, LB 2338 .D561
Music
   ML 100 .G883, ML 102, ML 1700-1711 (opera)
Native Americans
   E 75-78, E 89, PN 1995.9, Z 1209
Novels
   PN 3451
Philosophy
   B 51 .E56, B 29 .W681
Plays
   Z 5781 .C53, Z 5781 .O89, Z 5783 .P73, PR 625 .C7411
Poetry
   PN 4321 .G75, PR 502 .C851, Z 2014 .P7 A73
Politics
   JF, JK
Psychology
   BF 31, RC 334 .I5731, RC 455.2 .C4 A515
Quotations
   PN 6081
Religion
   BL 31, BX 841
Science
   Q 121 .M15
Science Fiction
   Z 5917 .S36 S2971 1987, PN 3433.5 .S331
Short Stories
   Z 5917 .S5 C77, Z 5917 .S5 W18 1977
Sociology
   HV 89 .S6, H 41 .E56
Speeches
   AI 3 .S97
Statistics
   HB 881 .A2 U5, HA 202 .A2, HA 441 .M62, HC 58 .U58, JX 1976
   .A1 Y3, HA 201,
   Z 7551 .S79, HA 40

Style Manuals
LB 2369 .T93 (Turabian), Z 253 .C532 (Chicago Manual of Style), PE 1478 .G43 (MLA), PN 171 .F56 S351 1985 (citing odd items), Z 7164 .G7 G371 (citing government documents)

Thesauruses
PE 1591

Women
CT 3260 .W63, Z 7961, Z 695.1, HQ 1115 .T871 1986

HISTORY AND RELATED SUBJECTS

Library of Congress Quick Classification Scheme for history and related subjects:

History of Civilization	CB
Chronologies	CE, D 2 - D 11
Heraldry	CR
Biography	CT
General History and Topography except Americas	D
Great Britain	DA
France	DC
Germany	DD
Classical Antiquity	DE
Soviet Union	DK
Turkey and the Balkan States	DR
Asia	DS
Africa	DT
American History (general)	E
Native Americans	E 51 - E 99
United States	E 151 - E 810
U.S. Local History	F 1 - F 970
Canada	F 1001 - F 1140
Latin America	F 1401 - F 3799

National Bibliographies (Z's):

United States	Z 1201 - 1999
Canada	Z 1365 - 1401
Latin America	Z 1461 - 1609
Europe	Z 2000 - 2959
British Isles	Z 2001 - 2089
France	Z 2161 - 2189
Asia, Africa, Australia	Z 3001 - 4941

Subject Bibliographies:

History	Z 6201 - 6209

Indexes and abstracts in the UGL that cover history:
Social Science Index
Public Affairs Information Service (PAIS)
United States Political Science Documents (USPSD)
Humanities Index

Two of the major indexes/abstracts, *America: History and Life* and *Historical Abstracts,* are not available at the UGL; however, they can be accessed on DIALOG and are available in paper format at the Graduate Library.

SUBJECT AREA HIGHLIGHTS

QA   Mathematics
     Books of math tables; includes computer science (after all, computers are really just mondo adding machines) and books about software.
QB   Astronomy
     atlases
QC   Physics

QD   Chemistry
     CRC Handbook of Chemistry and Physics QD 65 .C517h
QE   Earth Sciences/Geology
QH   Biological Science (general)
QK   Botany
QL   Zoology
R   Medical Science
     Some books aimed at the layperson on health in general and on illness; books on drugs ranging from *The Pill Book* (layperson's book) to *The Physician's Desk Reference* (physician's reference but readable) to the *Merck Index* (chemical formulas - highly technical). Includes Psychiatry.
S   Horticulture
     U.S. government agriculture statistics, plant identification books, gardening books
T   Technology
     Something of a grab-bag classification. Plain T covers general works. Includes *The Trade Names Dictionary,* way-things-work type of books
     TA   transportation
     TD   environment
     TJ   energy
     TL   space (as opposed to astronomy)
     TN   minerals
     TR   photography
     TT   fashion ??? (as opposed to costume, and please, don't ask cuz I don't know. Only 1 book there.)
     TX   cooking. *The Hotel/Motel Red Book,* a list (**not** comprehensive) of hotels around the country, is in the T's as well. Comes in handy but another of those "why is it **here**" puzzles.
U   Military Science
                       These last 2 do have a lot that falls under
                       "technology"
V   Naval Science

VII. SECONDARY TRAINING SESSIONS

BIOGRAPHICAL SOURCES IN THE UGL

The most obvious first stop is the *Who's Who*-type books. We have *Who's Who* (CT 770 .W6), *International Who's Who* (CT 103 .I63) and *Who's Who in America* (CT 210 .W63) as well a number of specialized volumes - women, midwest, etc. The UGL keeps only the most recent edition; the GL has many that we do not have and keeps the superceded editions in the regular stacks.

Current Biography (Ref CT 100 .C98) comes out monthly. Each issue indexes the current year. At the end of the year we receive an annual yearbook with entries in alphabetical order. Each annual indexes its own decade: 1971 indexes itself, 1975 indexes 1971-75 and 1980 indexes 1971-80. A separate index volume covers 1940 (vol. 1) - 1985. Entries are 1 - 5 pages long and illustrated, and each volume has an obituary section and a list of those included indexed by profession. It is international in scope.

Biography Index is a Wilson product. Each volume covers 2 years; the older ones cover 3. It includes not only magazines and journals indexed by other Wilson indexes, but some other serials and some books. It also has a listing by profession.

Biography and Genealogy Master Index is in three sections: the second edition, the 1981-85 cumulation and yearbooks since 1986. It has no authority control but gives one entry per spelling or birth date or initials used: see Zsa Zsa Gabor in volume 3 of the 2nd edition to see what kind of list one can have. The source abbreviations are very cryptic; the sources are spelled out on the inside front cover on pages that are an unfortunate violent yellow. Many of the references are for older editions of things we have; a good opportunity for an MCAT lesson.

Contemporary Authors and *Contemporary Authors New Revision* gives biographical information on writers of fiction, non-fiction, poetry, journalism, drama, motion pictures, and television. It includes writers in languages other than English if they have been translated or have been published in the U.S. Authors deceased since 1900 are included and the index is cumulative. *CANR* updates *CA,* but not volume for volume. The contents are also indexed in *CLC* and *TCLC*.

Other sources: *The Dictionary of American Biography* and *The Dictionary of National Biography* (British), encyclopedias (especially the very old Britannica for authors of the 19th century and earlier) and directories in subject areas (*APA Directory* or the *Dictionary of Contemporary Artists*).

For people currently in the news, *InfoTrac, Readers' Guide* and especially *National Newspaper Index* are frequently useful. *The New York Times* is a good source on new people in the government and for obituaries.

MIRLYN tips: for books about a person, do a subject search on the last name, then first name. "Biography" is a subheading, so it is a suitable keyword search term. Sometimes names vary in spelling and some authors use more than one name, so it is appropriate to check the name authority file in mcat. You must be in staff mode (ltul instead of luum). Type:

find na=

This is particularly useful when looking up names that do not come in the roman alphabet in the original. Like that guy in charge in Libya.

SCIENCE AND TECHNOLOGY SOURCES IN THE UGL

The UGL does not have a lot of science and technology material (call numbers Q-V) either in reference or in the circulating collection; the reference collection is **basic.** Which is not to say that it is easy; it is not appropriate for the junior high kid whose mom brought him in because *The World Book* wasn't technical enough on the subject of rocket construction (true story - I showed them what we had with the comment that it wasn't aimed at the layperson and that perhaps they'd be better off at the Public Library).

Encyclopedias and dictionaries:

The call number Q covers general science, hence that is where you find the *general* works. Each area has its own specialized works, of course.

The McGraw-Hill Encyclopedia of Science and Technology
Q 121 .M15 1987   20 volumes plus year books

Album of Science
class sep. but all in the Q's. Organized by eras.

Biography:

American Men and Women of Science
Q 141 .A49 1989/90   8 volumes   currently living

Dictionary of Scientific Biography
Q 141 .D55   16 volumes   history of science

Modern Scientists and Engineers
Q 141 .M15 1980   3 volumes

General biographical sources may also be used.

Indexes:

General Science Index and *Biological and Agricultural Index* are available in hard copy in the UGL; *GSI* is also in dwil.

Biology Digest - covers life sciences, includes abstracts.

Physical Fitness and Sports Medicine - medical orientation, highly technical, material mostly at Medical Library.

Bibliographies:

The UGL has very few science bibliographies (about 15, in 3 different call # areas in the Z's. A keyword search in MIRLYN using "bibliography.su." as one of the terms is a good start on a referral.

SOURCES IN THE UGL FOR SOCIAL SCIENCES OTHER THAN POLITICAL SCIENCE OR PSYCHOLOGY

The social sciences are frequently interdisciplinary but there are a couple of tools that cover the broad spectrum of the field.

Social Sciences Index (SSI) is the major index in the UGL for anthropology, area studies, community health, economics, geography, international relations, law and criminology, minority studies, planning and public administration, social work and public welfare and urban studies. It is available in paper or on dwil.

Social Sciences Citation Index (SSCI) is also very useful but can be something of a bear because it is huge, has teeny-tiny print and seems to have very few words completely spelled out. However, it has **excellent** guides on the inside front cover of each volume. And it does work; you really can find a complete citation using the sketchiest information, a boon when the article in question is older than the *SSI* computer data base. The *Permuterm Subject Index* lets you look up articles using two terms. It will refer you to authors whom you must then look up in the *Source Index*. These volumes list citations and the bibliographies of the articles, a useful way to find older, related research. No first names are used, only 1 or 2 initials, which can be frustrating when a patron is looking for all the articles he can find by John Smith! The titles of the articles and the types of journals listed can help determine which Smith, J you are really looking for. The *Citation Index* is a handy, dandy device for finding more information; it is in author order and lists people who have cited an article - a great way to find newer, related research. Warning: do not point at the index table and say "use that", especially with someone who is at all timid about the library. Take them and show them. Otherwise you could emotionally scar someone for life.

Other sources in the reference collection:

Call number H 41 includes *The Encyclopedia of Social Sciences, The International Encyclopedia of Social Sciences* and *The Dictionary of Social Sciences.* H - HC covers economics and statistical information. For searching in MIRLYN, a trip to *LCSH* may be in order first. "Social aspects" and "Economic aspects" are 2 common subheadings.

EDUCATION

Research Strategy:
1) Define and focus topic: be aware of interdisciplinary areas.
2) Little background material available, particularly in current theory but some things are available.
3) Use Education Index for small papers, CIJE for larger ones, and all of ERIC for extensive ones. Get current materials. Check bibliographies for germinal works and indexes in the field to follow up.
4) Fill in the gaps with other sources as needed: books and indexes in other fields, government studies, bibliographies.

Hints:
- People who want help choosing a school need access to objective information. If they insist on rankings, only Gourman does it regularly and he doesn't disclose his criteria.
- We get few education undergrads here so don't assume anything about how much knowledge the patron may posess.
- We do have some material on UM.

Books:
ERIC, L901's. *Encyclopedia of Education*, Buros, LB 2338's. *Encyclopedia of Special Education, Commonwealth Universities Yearbook*, Z 5811 - 5817, *Tests in Print*.

LITERATURE

Watch out for these things:
1) Undergraduate students are pretty unsophisticated about the variety of information available about literature. They don't know, even more so than usual, how to ask for what they need. Careful, thorough reference interviewing can save you lots of wasted time.
2) Confusion about terms is common here, too. A patron asking for a "review" of a work of literature (or a "book review") may be looking for any one of a number of things. Again, the reference interview is very important.

Most common information needs at the UGL and where to start looking:
1) Book reviews:
   Book Review Index
   Book Review Digest
2) Information about an author and his or her work:
   Contemporary Authors
   Dictionary of Literary Biography
   Current Biography, BGMI (these two are less helpful)
3) A small amount of information about a particular work:
   An edition of the work with a critical introduction
   Masterplots
   Magill's (various titles)
   Books about the author
   Twentieth Century Short Story Explication
4) Extensive information about a particular author and/or work:

Books about the author (check bibliographies, too)
Contemporary Literary Criticism
Twentieth Century Literary Criticism
MLA International Bibliography

HISTORY

Stuff to keep in mind:
1) Interdisciplinary nature of subject - the study of history includes the areas of political science, economics, geography, statistics, biography and the social sciences.
2) Does the patron want factual information, such as dates of specific events, or bibliographic sources?
3) Conduct the reference interview carefully. Some of the questions you might consider asking the patron include:
   a) What other areas of study (see those listed above) apply to the topic?
   b) What specific geographic region is being covered?
   c) What time frame is being covered?
   d) Has the patron read any background information on the subject?
   e) Are primary or secondary sources needed?
   f) Is biographical information needed?

Some basic reference tools:
General encyclopedias, such as the *Americana* and *World Book*, will provide you with very broad overviews of any country's history and major events. Begin with one of these if the patron knows very little about the subject.

Cambridge Ancient History	D 57 .C178 1983
Cambridge Medieval History	D 117 .C78
New Cambridge Modern History	D 208 .N52
Dictionary of American History	E 174 .D55 1976
Great Events from History	
American Series	E 178 .M221
Ancient and Medieval Series	D 59 .M261
Modern European Series	D 209 .M291
Worldwide 20th Century Series	D 421 .G631
Atlas of American History	G 1201 .S1 F41 1987
Harper Atlas of World History	G 1031 .G685131987
Documents of American History	E 173 .C73 1988
Historical Statistics of the U.S.	HA 202 .A2 1976

Interdisciplinary sources:

Europa Yearbook	D 2 .E92
Whitakers Almanac	AY 754 .W6
Facts on File	D 410 .F14
Keesing's Contemporary Archives	D 410 .K263
Asia and Pacific Review	HC 411 .A82
Latin America 1988	F 1410 .L354
Middle East Review	HC 410.7 .M62

PSYCHOLOGY

Stuff to watch out for:
1) When you get students with questions in psychology, be sure to find out the following during the reference interview:
   a. Does the student have adequate background information? If not, then try to get the patron to read some of the material in the reference collection. See the handout of basic sources.
   b. Is the topic too broad or too narrow? Again, try to get the patron to do some preliminary research in the reference collection.
      One great way to narrow the amount of citations one gets in PsycINFO is to use the descriptor LITERATURE-REVIEW along with the main subject. This limits the citations one gets considerably, and it sometimes provides the patron with good background information.
   c. Is the subject interdisciplinary?
      Psychology is one of those areas of study that overlaps with a great many others, especially sociology, education and the biological sciences.
      Try, during the reference interview, to ascertain what disciplines pertain to the subject being covered. Also, be careful to find out whether or not the subject has anything to do with medicine or psychiatry. Many of our reference books in psychology, as well as those in psychiatry, are kept in the R's. Be sure to check there as well when recommending background sources to the patron.
2) If you get a patron who has done quite a bit of research already, you may want to recommend some off the research guides that are in the reference collection. *How to Find Out in Psychology* and *Research Guide to Psychology* are a couple of the better, more advanced ones that you should keep in mind.
3) Keep in mind, as well, that there are lots of bibliographies related to psychology in the reference collection. For example, we have some excellent titles on suicide, homosexuality, television and drugs, all in the Z's.
4) If you find that there is a rather long line at the PsycLit terminal, inform some of the patrons that the *Social Sciences Index* on dwil also covers psychology. Although coverage of the subject isn't as extensive, SSI does index the major psychological journals published in this country.

INDEXES

General tips:
1) Help people understand the difference between a magazine and a journal. Don't assume they know the difference or its importance.
2) Use our annotated Sheehy's Guide to Reference Books to refer people elsewhere. Be sure that they have a specific index title and that the library is indeed still getting it.
3) Paper indexes are great for teaching basics so don't assume people need a computer.
4) Be sure to have a patron interpret a citation before you leave him/her whenever possible.

Table 2B   Sciences

Physical Fitness/Sports Medicine - good index, no abstracts, more scholarly than "hot" topics

General Science Index - on dwil, more medicine than might be expected

Biological and Agricultural Index - standard Wilson index, some environmental data

Table 2A and part of Table 1B   Reviews, Movies and Plays

New York Times Theatre Reviews - collection of reviews from NYT; must use the papers themselves for more recent years

Film Literature Index - international coverage, good subject access

Variety Film Reviews - collection of reviews from Variety, don't have last few years yet

New York Times Film Reviews - collection of reviews from NYT

Rest of Table 1B   Humanities

Humanities Index - interdisciplinary, some of several areas, we have full paper set, also on dwil

Essay and General Literature Index - covers more literature and arts than HI, also has ethics and philosophy

MLA International Bibliography - good international coverage, try other 2 first though as this is harder to use, subject index, changed format in 1981, available on CD-Rom at GL

Table 1A   Political Science

PAIS - books, journal articles and government documents on public policy; available on MIRLYN (gov. docs are not yet cataloged on MCAT)

USPSD - many journals, some documents, scholarly, U.S. focus, subject and author indexes

CIS - changed format in 1986, sends people to a fiche set in the Grad Microform Room, has legislative histories

Table 3A   Potpourri

ASI - refers people to fiche in Grad, American statistics, not just from the government, has an international counterpart in the GL

Biography Index - Wilson, articles on people, latest year could index an article on someone who died centuries ago, so always check all volumes, includes books

Biography and Genealogy Master Index - be sure to check supplements as well as base sets, leads you to books which have info on people. A volume of base set has been annotated to show which ones we have and where they are; older editions of many *Who's Who* type books at GL

Index to Black Periodicals - arranged like Readers' Guide, now focuses on Black periodicals, but used to have slightly broader coverage, useful, scholarly

Table 3B   Potpourri

Readers' Guide - **not** on dwil, is on CD-ROM by itself

Women's Studies Abstracts - covers all disciplines as they relate to women

Communications Abstracts - good abstracts

New York Times - basic newspaper index, remember to consider using National Newspaper Index instead, does not number the sections of the paper the same way the paper does and can be VERY confusing to the user

Table 4A   Education and Social Sciences

Child Development Abstracts and Bibliography - good for this area but not
    comprehensive
Exceptional Child Education Resources - advanced but useful
Social Sciences Citation Index - remember 5 year cumulations, use instructions
    in front of book as needed, rarely a first choice
Social Science Index - on dwil

Table 5A   Education

Resources in Education - part of ERIC, documents in MMR at GL, no quality
    control, use thesaurus, good abstracts
CIJE - part of ERIC, comprehensive coverage of education journals, brief
    abstracts
Education Index - a Wilson index

Table 4B   Psychology

Psychological Abstracts - see handout, be sure you can do this easily

Table 5B

Sociological Abstracts - poor subject access, decent abstracts, more useful at
    GL in computer format

VI. EXERCISES

Name_____

Return to_____by_____

ONLINE EXERCISE

Search MIRLYN Public Mode (a.k.a the opac):lnav, and MIRLYN Staff Mode: ltul. Try to find the following items. Write down your search statement for each. CLUE: you may or may not use the same search for each mode. It depends.

1. Find a biography of John Cheever.

   lnav:_____
   ltul:_____
   call# of the first book:_____

2. Find a book titled CONTEMPORARY CHICANO FICTION.

   lnav:_____
   ltul:_____
   who has it:_____

3. Find the Russian newspaper PRAVDA.

   lnav:_____
   ltul:_____
   how many print versions does the library have:_____
   what dates are covered by the microfilm version(s):_____

4. How do you find the correct Library of Congress (LC) spelling of Muammar Ghaddafi's name?

   lnav:_____
   ltul:_____
   how *do* the sages at Library of Congress spell it?_____

5. Find the book with the ISBN 0-300-03709-0.

   lnav:_____

   ltul:_____

   So, what is it? (title or call#):_____

6. How many books have "homes and haunts" as a Library of Congress subtitle?

   lnav:_____

   ltul:_____

   The Magic Number:_____

7. Your patron is in a tizzy because she has a call number and can't remember what book it's for!

   It's PS 3558 .A65 B7 1976

   lnav:_____

   ltul:_____

   name of the book:_____

ONLINE EXERCISE ANSWERS

Search MIRLYN Public Mode (a.k.a the opac):lnav, and MIRLYN Staff Mode: ltul. Try to find the following items. Write down your search statement for each. CLUE: you may or may not use the same search for each mode. It depends.

1. Find a biography of John Cheever.
   lnav: **s=cheever john--biography**
   ltul: **fi js=cheever john -biography**
   call# of the book: **828 C5130 C51**

2. Find a book titled CONTEMPORARY CHICANO FICTION.
   lnav: **t=contemporary chicano fiction**
   ltul: **fi jt=contemporary chicano fiction**
   who has it: **gl**

3. Find the Russian newspaper PRAVDA.
   lnav: **t pravda**
   ltul: **jt pravda**
   how many print versions does the library have: **2 English and Russian**
   what dates are covered by the microfilm version(s): **1917-**

4. How do you find the correct LC spelling of Muammar Ghaddafi's name?
   lnav: **a=ghaddafi gives "search under" reference**
   ltul: **fn=ghaddafi**
   how *do* the sages at LC spell it? **Qaddafi**

5. Find the book with the ISBN 0-300-03709-0.
   lnav: **k 0300037090 (no spaces or dashes)**
   ltul: **fi nb=the number with or without the dashes**
   So, what is it? (title or call#): **DS 119.7 .M561 1988 The PLO under Arafat**

6. How many books have "homes and haunts" as a Library of Congress subtitle?
   lnav: **k=homes.su. haunts.su. (or just haunts.su.)**
   ltul: **can't do**
   The Magic Number: **931 as of 9/9/91**

7. Your patron is in a tizzy because she has a call number and can't remember what book it's for!
   It's PS 3558 .A65 B7 1976
   lnav: **c ps 3558 a 65 b 7 1976**
   ltul: **fi cl=ps 3558 a 65 b 7 1975**
   name of the book: **blood on the bosom devine**

Name_____

Return to_____by_____

ACCESS EXERCISE

Controlled vocabulary, thesauri and winging it:

1. Using *LSCH* (*Library of Congress Subject Headings*), find the subject heading for books on writing headlines for newspapers.

2. "I, uh, like, want to write, ya know, on *really old* people, like 70 or so who drink so much they see, uh, pink elephants?" What <u>subject headings</u> would you use to do a keyword search PSYC on MIRLYN.

    How about for *really really old* people, like 90?

3. AIDS affects all aspects of life and is generally given one of two subject headings: AIDS (Disease) or Acquired Immune Deficiency Syndrome. Who uses which?

	AIDS...	Acquired....
MCAT	_____	_____
MCAT sm	_____	_____
DWIL	_____	_____
PSYC	_____	_____
PAIS	_____	_____
Sociological Abstracts	_____	_____
Women's Studies Abst	_____	_____
ERIC	_____	_____
Essay & General Lit	_____	_____
New York Times	_____	_____

4. The Amazon is being denuded of trees. What subject heading would you use for this phenomenon?

    MCAT _____

    DWIL _____

    PAIS _____

5. Where can you find subject headings for DWIL databases?

MCAT

6. How can you find material on Southern California?

7. What library on campus has a journal called *The Unspeakable Visions by the Individual* or something like that? Can I get volume 8? What is the journal about?

8. Which libraries on campus have volume 12 and/or volume 14 of the *NAJE Educator*?

9. The Social Work Library has holdings for the *Journal of Homosexuality*. List their holdings by volume and issue number.

DWIL

10. If you do the search *s=drug testing* you will get articles only from *Social Sciences Index*. What should you do to get articles from other indexes in dwil? Name 2 of these other headings.

11. Your patron is researching the downfall of Richard Nixon. She can find information under *Watergate Affair* and *Watergate Case* but nothing from the time that it happened. Why?

12. Do a subject search on deforestation. Is the article "Adios Amazonia" available? What would you tell an undergraduate who had sort of planned ahead: the paper is due in 3 days.

PSYC

13. How do you find articles by Johnson and Smith?

14. How do you find an article titled something like "Laughing in the Face of Death" or "Laugh at the Face of Death"? What is the correct title?

15. How do you find articles using the subject terms *adolescence* and *risk taking*? How many are there?

PAIS

16. Do the search *s=egypt* and look at #1. Who owns *The Blood of Abraham*? What is the call number?

17. Do the search *s=World Health Organization*. Look at the first index list. What information is needed to find "Coping with AIDS: three years into the WHO program on AIDS" in the library?

ACCESS ANSWERS

Controlled vocabulary, thesauri and winging it:

1. Using *LSCH* (*Library of Congress Subject Headings*), find the subject
    heading for books on writing headlines for newspapers.
    newspapers--headlines

2. "I, uh, like, want to write, ya know, on *really old* people, like 70 or so
    who drink so much they see, uh, pink elephants?" What subject
    headings would you use to do a keyword search PSYC on MIRLYN.
    alcoholic psychosis   aged
    How about for *really really old* people, like 90?   **very old**

3. AIDS affects all aspects of life and is generally given one of two subject
    headings: AIDS (Disease) or Acquired Immune Deficiency Syndrome.
    Who uses which?

	AIDS...	Acquired....
MCAT	___x___	_____
MCAT sm	_____	___x__
DWIL	___x___	_____
PSYC	_____	___x__
PAIS	_____	___x__
Sociological Abstracts	_____	___x__
Women's Studies Abst	_____	___x__
ERIC	___x___	_____
Essay & General Lit	___x___	_____
New York Times	_____	___x__

4. The Amazon is being denuded of trees. What subject heading would you
    use for this phenomenon?
    MCAT: **deforestation**
    DWIL: **deforestation**
    PAIS: **clearcutting**

5. Where can you find subject headings for DWIL databases?
    **in the paper copies or by doing a keyword search and
    looking at headings on useful articles**

MCAT

6. How can you find material on Southern California?
    k=california.su. southern.su.

7. What library on campus has a journal called *The Unspeakable Visions by
    the Individual* or something like that? Can I get volume 8? What is the
    journal about?
    GL, no, American literature

8.   Which libraries on campus have volume 12 and/or volume 14 of the
     NAJE Educator?
     Music library has vol. 12; stopped before getting 14

9.   The Social Work Library has holdings for the *Journal of Homosexuality*.
     List their holdings by volume and issue number.
     vol 7, #4,   vol 7, #2-3, and vol 6, #4

DWIL

10. If you do the search *s=drug testing* you will get articles only from Social
     Sciences Index. What should you do to get articles from other indexes in
     dwil? Name 2 of these other headings.
     k=drug test$,   drug abuse testing,   drug abuse-testing

11. Your patron is researching the downfall of Richard Nixon. She can find
     information under *Watergate Affair* and *Watergate Case* but nothing from
     the time that it happened. Why?
     coverage begins in 1983

12. Do a subject search on deforestation. Is the article "Adios Amazonia"
     available? What would you tell an undergraduate who had sort of
     planned ahead: the paper is due in 3 days.
     **Only 1986 available on campus, interlibrary loan takes
     several days.**

PSYC

13. How do you find articles by Johnson and Smith?
     k=johnson.au. and smith.au.

14. How do you find an article titled something like "Laughing in the Face of
     Death" or "Laugh at the Face of Death"? What is the correct title?
     k=laugh$ face death,   "To Laugh in the Face of Death"

15. How do you find articles using the subject terms *adolescence* and *risk
     taking*? How many are there?
     k=adolescence.su. and (risk adj taking).su.,   83

PAIS

16. Do the search *s=egypt* and look at #1. Who owns *The Blood of
     Abraham*? What is the call number?
     GL, UGL,   DS63.1 .C371 1985

17. Do the search *s=World Health Organization*. Look at the first index list.
     What information is needed to find "Coping with AIDS: three years into
     the WHO program on AIDS" in the library?
     **SD (Superintendent of Documents) cat no, Y 4.F 76/1:Aug
     5/2**

Name_____

Return to_____by_____

CD ROM EXERCISES

Use the BROWSE and WILSEARCH modes of Readers' Guide, InfoTrac and ProQuest (if it's up and running and has proper coverage) to find information on reaction to the selection of Dan Quayle as the Vice Presidential nominee. Write down your search strategy (both your great and not-so-great efforts) for each tool and describe your results. Hint: this is one of those nasty things that have no single correct answer but lots of *good* answers so let your imagination run riot. Attach printouts if you like.

Readers' Guide BROWSE:

Readers' Guide WILSEARCH:

Readers' Guide WILSONLINE:

InfoTrac:

Name_____

Return to_____by_____

PERIODICAL INDEX PRACTICE

For each of the subjects below, determine which paper periodical index in the UGL would be most appropriate and list the subject heading(s) and subheading(s) you used.   If more than one index would work for the question, note your first choice and why it is your first choice.   Hand the results to your supervisor.

RULES & USEFUL HINTS: 1) don't use indexes that are duplicated on computers here [dwil indexes, Readers' Guide, InfoTrac, PAIS, Pscyh Abst. etc];   2) not all paper indexes are covered with this exercise;   3) no index is the correct answer to more than one question;   4) of course, we are fishing for a particular answer but there are some right wrong answers.

A patron comes to the desk and says:

1.   I'm looking for scholarly articles on acid rain in relationship to farming.

   index:_____

   subject headings:_____

2.   I want to compare employment of blacks as teachers in 1955, 1975, 1990.

   index:_____

   subj head 1955:_____

   subj head 1975:_____

   subj head 1990:_____

3.   I need some literary criticism of Stephen J. Gould's *The Mismeasure of Man*. It was published in 1982. (This is a trick question.)

   index:_____

   subj head:_____

   what is the trick:_____

4.   My professor told me to find an article that was published in a journal in 1989 about Sylvia Plath. She can't remember the author's name.

   index:_____

   subj head:_____

5. I'm looking for scholarly articles on testing bias of all sorts in SATs and other such tests.

    index:_____

    subj head_____

6. I need criticism, not reviews, of the films of Michelangelo Antonioni.

    index:_____

    subj head:_____

7. I'm looking for stuff on athletes using drugs.   Stuff on how it screws up their bodies.

    index:_____

    subj head:_____

8. I need to know about who is likely to vote and why.

    index:_____

    subj head:_____

9. With all this Kennedy and Palm Beach stuff and publishing rape victims' names and stuff I want to find out about what it's moral for reporters to write about.

    index:_____

    subj head:_____

PERIODICAL INDEX ANSWERS

For each of the subjects below, determine which paper periodical index in the UGL would be most appropriate and list the subject heading(s) and subheading(s) you used.   If more than one index would work for the question, note your first choice and why it is your first choice.   Hand the results to your supervisor.

USEFUL HINTS: 1) don't use indexes that are duplicated on computers here [dwil indexes, Readers' Guide, InfoTrac, PAIS, Pscyh Abst. etc];   2) not all paper indexes are covered with this exercise;   3) no index is the correct answer to more than one question; 4) of course, we are fishing for a particular answer but there are some right wrong answers.

A patron comes to the desk and says:

1. I'm looking for scholarly articles on acid rain in relationship to farming.
   index: **Bio and Ag**
   subject headings: **acid rain--effect on soils**

2. I want to compare employment of blacks as teachers in 1955, 1975, 1990.
   index: Educ Index
   subj head 1955: **Negro teachers**
   subj head 1975: **Negro teachers**
   subj head 1990: **Black teachers**

3. I need some literary criticism of Stephen J. Gould's *The Mismeasure of Man*. It was published in 1982. (This is a trick question.)
   index: **Book Review Index   1982**
   subj head: **author name**
   what is the trick: **people sometimes call reviews of non-literature "literary criticism"**

4. My professor told me to find an article that was published in a journal in 1989 about Sylvia Plath. She can't remember the author's name.
   index: **mla**
   subj head: **Plath, Sylvia**

5. I'm looking for scholarly articles on testing bias of all sorts in SATs and other such tests.
   index: **ERIC**
   subj head: **test bias**

6. I need criticism, not reviews, of the films of Michelangelo Antonioni.
   index: **Film Literature Index**
   subj head: **Antonioni or individual film titles**

7. I'm looking for stuff on athletes using drugs.   Stuff on how it screws up their bodies.
    index: **Physical Fitness/Sports Medicine**
    subj head: **anabolic steroids**

8. I need to know about who is likely to vote and why.
    index: **USPSD**
    subj head: **voter turnout,   voter behavior**

9. With all this Kennedy and Palm Beach stuff and publishing rape victims' names and stuff I want to find out about what it's moral for reporters to write about.
    index: **Communication Abstracts**
    subj head: **ethics**

REFERENCE INTERVIEW EXERCISE

Please complete this sheet during your desk hours and return it to your supervisor within one week. If you have any questions, just ask at any time.

1. What are two things you taught patrons while at the reference or computer desk? How did you do this teaching?

2. Name two examples of your efforts to practice proactive reference. Which was more effective? Do you have any further ideas in this area?

3. Name two things you do to create or maintain good patron relations. Have you observed any other means of accomplishing this end?

4. Write down everything you did on each of two more complex reference questions. What strategy did you use? What tools? How did you find out whether or not the patron was really satisfied with what you did?

   a)

   b)

REFERENCE RUNAROUND EXERCISE

Your answer will take the form of the **sources** used to find the information. Return the completed sheet to your supervisor. You are expected to have questions about some of these so feel free to ask for assistance from the staff and discuss the questions with your peers.

1. I need an overview of recent critical thought on the works of Gabriel Garcia Marquez. Find the best source.

2. Who is the governor of Minnesota?

3. I need a source that gives me biographical information on Jesse Jackson.

4. I need a book review of the book *The Closing of the American Mind.*

5. Where can I find the address to the United States Embassy in Mexico?

6. What is the address of the U.S. Copyright Office?

7. How many kilometers are there in a mile?

8. What's been going on in South Africa in the last few years? I need a summary, something I could read in less than one hour.

9. Now I need an overview of South Africa's history---something I can read in an hour or so. Plus I need a list of current government officials and their addresses.

10. How many people died in car accidents in Michigan, Indiana, and Ohio in the last few years?

11. I want to know how Senator Bentsen voted on some key issues, how lobby groups rate him, and how he financed his latest campaigns.

12. Is information about graduate business schools available? Where?

13. What is the origin and history of the use of the word "amuse"?

14. Where did the phrase "blood, sweat, and tears" come from?

15. What's a quark? I need a fairly sophisticated overview.

16. I need something that gives constants and formulas for chemistry.

17. What's the inflation rate of the U.S. been in the last five or so years?

18. What is the address of Totes, Inc.?

19. I'm trying to find out about Plessy vs. Ferguson. Is there a source that I could look at that would give me a brief overview?

20. What graduate schools have physical therapy programs?

REFERENCE RUNAROUND ANSWERS

Remember to make note of your answers and return the completed sheet to your supervisor. You are expected to have questions about some of these so feel free to ask for assistance from the staff and discuss the questions with your peers.

1. I need an overview of recent critical thought on the works of Gabriel Garcia Marquez. Find the best source.
   CLC

2. Who is the governor of Minnesota?
   Information Please or any other almanac

3. I need a source that gives me biographical information on Jesse Jackson.
   Current Biography, Who's Who

4. I need a book review of the book *The Closing of the American Mind*.
   Book Review Index

5. Where can I find the address to the United States Embassy in Mexico?
   Europa Yearbook

6. What is the address of the U.S. Copyright Office?
   U.S. Government Manual

7. How many kilometers are there in a mile?
   almanac

8. What's been going on in South Africa in the last few years? I need a summary, something I could read in less than one hour.
   Africa South of the Sahara, South Africa

9. Now I need an overview of South Africa's history---something I can read in an hour or so. Plus I need a list of current government officials and their addresses.
   same as 8

10. How many people died in car accidents in Michigan, Indiana, and Ohio in the last few years?
    Accident Facts

11. I want to know how Senator Bentsen voted on some key issues, how lobby groups rate him, and how he financed his latest campaigns.
    Politics in America, Almanac of American Politics

12. Is information about graduate business schools available? Where?
    Barron's Guide to B Schools and
    Business Week's Schools

13.   What is the origin and history of the use of the word "amuse"?
      Oxford England Dictionary (OED)

14.   Where did the phrase "blood, sweat, and tears" come from?
      Bartlett's

15.   What's a quark? I need a fairly sophisticated overview.
      McGraw-Hill Encyc. of Science and Technology

16.   I need something that gives constants and formulas for chemistry.
      CRC Handbook

17.   What's the inflation rate of the U.S. been in the last five or so years?
      Statistical Abstracts

18.   What is the address of Totes, Inc.?
      Standard and Poor

19.   I'm trying to find out about Plessy vs. Ferguson. Is there a source that
      I could look at that would give me a brief overview?
      Guide to American Law

20.   What graduate schools have physical therapy programs?
      Peterson's Guide to Graduate Programs

Appendix 2

Undergraduate Library Minority Student User Survey

Background information:
(1)   (check *one* below)

    1. ___   Freshman
    2. ___   Sophomore
    3. ___   Junior
    4. ___   Senior
    5. ___   Other

(2)   (check *one* below)

    1. ___   Black
    2. ___   Hispanic American
    3. ___   Asian American
    4. ___   Native American/American Indian
    5. Other

(3)   (check *one* below)

    1. ___   male
    2. ___   female

(4) Major (intended major) department _____

* *

How often do you use the following facilities, for any purpose?
(circle *one* number in each category)

		very often	often	some-times	rarely	never
5.	Undergraduate Library	1	2	3	4	5
6.	Graduate Library	1	2	3	4	5
7.	dorm library?	1	2	3	4	5
8.	Other library (*please specify_____*)	1	2	3	4	5
9.	Microcomputer Center at the UGL	1	2	3	4	5

(10)   **What library do you usually prefer to use, for any purpose?** (check *one*)

    1. ____   Undergraduate Library

    2. ____   Graduate Library

    3. ____   Dorm library

    4. ____   Other library (*please specify_____*)

Why do you prefer the library checked in question #10? (check *all* that apply)

    11. ____   Convenience of location

    12. ____   Usually has the books/materials I want

    13. ____   Staff is most helpful

    14. ____   Hours are convenient

    15. ____   Quieter environment

    16. ____   Less crowded

    17. ____   Other (*please specify_____*)

How often do you do the following activities at the Undergraduate Library? (circle *one* number in each category)

		very often	often	some- times	rarely	never
18.	Study/do research using my own materials	1	2	3	4	5
19.	Study/do research using library materials	1	2	3	4	5
20.	Meet friends	1	2	3	4	5
21.	Find non-class-related reading such as novels or newspapers	1	2	3	4	5
22.	Use the Reserve Service (books and other materials reserved for classes)	1	2	3	4	5
23.	Use the Microcomputer Center	1	2	3	4	5
24.	Consult with someone on the reference staff	1	2	3	4	5
25.	Other (please specify_____)	1	2	3	4	5

How often do you consult with someone in the Reference Department at the Undergraduate Library (located on the 1st floor, just inside the glass doors past the stairs) for the following? (circle *one* number in each category)

		very often	often	some-times	rarely	never
26.	For directions around the building or campus	1	2	3	4	5
27.	For research assistance, finding material for papers, assignments, etc.	1	2	3	4	5
28.	For help in using indexes, the card catalog, GEAC, reference books, etc.	1	2	3	4	5
29.	Other (please specify_____)	1	2	3	4	5

If, in the above question, you circled "rarely" or "never" two or more times, please answer the following question. What is the reason you generally rarely or never consult with the Reference staff? (check *all* that apply)

30. ____ I don't feel I need it

31. ____ I wasn't aware of the possibility

32. ____ Reference staff is not around when I need them

33. ____ Had a bad experience previously
   (*please describe on the back of this page*)

34. ____ Other (*please specify_____*)

(35) When you consult with the Reference staff, are questions generally answered to your satisfaction?

1. ____ Yes

2. ____ No

Comments?

Please rate the Undergraduate Library for: (circle *one* number in each category)

		very often	often	some-times	rarely	never
36.	Staff helpfulness	1	2	3	4	5
37.	Study space	1	2	3	4	5
38.	Hours	1	2	3	4	5
39.	Availability of materials I need	1	2	3	4	5
40.	Comfortable environment	1	2	3	4	5

(41) **What time of day do you usually use the Undergraduate Library?** (check *one*)

1. ____ morning (8-12)   2. ____ afternoon (12-5)

3. ____ evening (5-10)   4. ____ night (10-closing)

(42) **Have you ever heard of the Peer Information Counseling Program (PIC) (a peer counseling program designed to help minority students on a one-to-one basis in using the library and microcomputer center)?**

1. ____ yes   2. ____ no

If you answered "yes" in question 42, please answer questions 43-53. If you answered "no", please skip to question 54.

How did you learn of the PIC program? From a... (check *all* that apply)

43. ____ Flyer

44. ____ Friend

45. ____ Library staff member

46. ____ Academic or other University counselor

47. ____ Other (*please specify*_____)

Which of the following services have you received from the PIC program? (check *all* that apply)

48. ____ Term paper counseling/individual research assistance

49. ____ Library lecture, talk

50. ____ Microcomputer training

51. ____ Other (*please specify*_____)

52. ____ None

(53)   In general, how would you rate the service(s) you received
       from the PIC program? (check *one*)

    1. ____   excellent   2. ____   good

    3. ____   fair   4. ____   poor

    5. ____   very poor   6. ____   I have never used
                                                the PIC program

(54)   In general, do you feel the Undergraduate Library meets
       your needs as a minority student?

    1. ____   yes   2. ____   no

(55)   What can the Undergraduate Library do for you to enhance
       your educational experience here at the University of
       Michigan?

Thank you for participating in this survey!

Appendix 3

Advertisements

Undergraduate Library
Ann Arbor, MI 48109-1185
(313) 763-5084

University Library
The University of Michigan   Ann Arbor, Michigan 48109

September 10, 1990

Dear First Year Student,

Greetings from the Undergraduate Library!

As Peer Information Counseling students, we would like to welcome you to
Ann Arbor, The University of Michigan, and the Undergraduate Library.
Peer Information Counseling (PIC) is a program here at the UGLi
especially for undergraduate students. We are here to make you feel more
comfortable with using our library's many resources. We are all
undergraduate students, just like you, and we remember how intimidating
a huge library seemed at first. As PIC students, we are ready at the
Reference Desk to answer any question you may have! No question is too
small or large...try us!

As a new student, the best thing you can do is come on in to the UGLi as
soon as possible and find out what we have to offer. We will show you
how to use MIRLYN -- the library's online catalog and indexes; we will
show you where the copiers are, where the journals and magazines
are located...we can show you everything you will need!

In addition to showing you around the library, we can also teach you how
to do wordprocessing on a Zenith or Macintosh computer. We will take
as much time as you need to learn the basics of Microsoft Word, or help
you brush up on rusty computer skills.

Remember, we were all new on this large campus at one time. Learning
how to use the library for research and study has helped us more than we
can express. The library can be your ticket to better grades, and we can
help you master the library! So, come by and see us. If you have any
questions about PIC, give us a call at 764-4479, or call 764-6849 and
leave a message.

Sincerely,

Veenu Aulakh   Carolyn A Bryant   Rakesh Patel
Cristina S. Barroso   Kacee Stan   Edward Pretzl
Karen E. Downing (coordinator)

Peer Information Counselors

Exhibit 1. PIC Letter. This letter is enclosed in a newsletter sent to all undergraduate first-year minority students.

PIC News

Peer Information Counseling   The University of Michigan Undergraduate Library   Winter 1991

The Peer Information Counseling Program is a minority student support program brought to you by the University of Michigan Undergraduate Library. We're here to help make using the library a little easier. Looking for some information for a term paper? Or need a little help using MIRLYN? Perhaps you'd like someone to take the time to show you how to do basic word-processing on Microsoft Word. That's what we're here for!

We're looking for a few good folks!

Would you like to join us? PIC is looking for new staff to start in the Fall term of 1991. Working for PIC offers the opportunity to meet and help people as well as to learn many useful skills. See page 4 if you are interested.

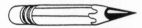

PIC NEWS
is a publication of
Peer Information
Counseling
The University of Michigan
Undergraduate Library
Ann Arbor, MI 48109-1185
PIC-Line: 764-6849
Coordinator: 764-4479
PIC News Editors:
Karen Downing
Barbara Hoppe

MAKE THE MOST OF MIRLYN!

Many students don't realize there is an important difference between SUBJECT and KEYWORD searching when using MIRLYN. This difference is so important that it can affect whether or not you find what you are looking for in MIRLYN.

When doing a SUBJECT search in MCAT, you MUST use the *Library of Congress Subject Headings* (LCSH). This is a giant list of subject terms that has been compiled by librarians at the Library of Congress in Washington, D.C. This means you CANNOT just sit down to a terminal and start typing in subject terms as you think of them. Rather, you must find the large red books that are kept at the Reference Desk and by the MIRLYN terminals, and look up the LCSH terminology.

When doing KEYWORD searching, you do not have to use the LCSH terminology. You can play around with your own terminology to see if you can find any books or articles on your topic. Keyword searches take a little longer to run than subject searches because the computer is searching the entire record (author, title, subject, publisher, place of publication fields) of the book or article. When you do a Subject search, the computer searches only the subject field.

The same principles apply to the other databases. For PSYC, use the *Thesaurus of Psychological Index Terms*; for PAIS, use *PAIS Subject Headings*. The six indexes in DWIL do not use uniform subject headings and publisher does not provide any guide to headings.

For more information on the differences between SUBJECT and KEYWORD searching, please stop by the Reference Desk on the main floor of the Undergraduate Library. And, if you find as you are searching MIRLYN that you are not finding the information you need, please stop and ask for help at the Reference Desk! Chances are, we can show you a different way to search, which will turn up all sorts of information.

Exhibit 2. PIC Newsletter. Released twice per year (in the fall term and in the winter term), this four-page newsletter is available in the reference area, and is mailed out to all undergraduates of color, as well as to individuals and departments on a comprehensive mailing list.

"PIC"

THIS

UP

and turn it over

We are PIC. . . .

Peer Information Counselors
at the Undergraduate Library.
And we'd like to invite you to
come by and use "PIC"
services.

We can help you find information and research materials in
the library.

We can also get you started
on word processing. It's easy.
And it doesn't take long to
learn.

Drop by the Undergraduate
Library Reference Desk, on
the first floor, or call 764-4479
for more information.

We're finished. You can turn
it over again now.

 **Peer
Information
Counseling**

Exhibit 3. PIC Bookmark (front and back).

 Peer Information Counseling
    University of Michigan
    Undergraduate Library
    764-4479

                                    PIC Assistant

    Information is Empowerment

Exhibit 4. Business cards, given to all Peer
Information Counselors to distribute as appropriate.

PEER INFORMATION COUNSELING PROGRAM (PIC) MATERIALS FOR U OF M FACULTY

One of the goals of the Peer Information Counseling Program (PIC) is to familiarize students with research concepts in a comfortable environment. PIC offers special handouts to introduce new students to the library. Each handout encourages independent explorations of the library. If you would like some PIC handouts for yourself or for your students, please complete and return this form, indicating quantities needed.

Reference Works on People of Color

Selected bibliographies found in the UGLi on People of Color

____ Reference Works on Asian Americans

____ Reference Works on African Americans

____ Reference Works on Latino Americans

____ Reference Works on Native Americans

Research Guides

____ A Guide to Researching Black History

____ A Guide to Researching Martin Luther King, Jr.

Did You Knows

Brief biographical paragraphs on important people of color

African-Americans:
____ John James Audubon
____ Alexa Canady
____ Charles Hamilton Houston
____ Leontyne Price
____ Mary Ann Shadd
____ William Monroe Trotter

Latino Americans:
____ Joan Baez
____ Cesar Chavez
____ Angela De Hoyas
____ Diego Rivera

Important Woman Scientists:
____ Katherine Burr Blodgett
____ Florence Peebles
____ Sarah Francis Whiting

Asian Americans:
____ Daniel Akaka
____ Carlos Bulosan
____ Wu Chien-Shiung
____ Ch'iu Chin
____ Daniel Inouye
____ Yamasaki Minorou

Native Americans:
____ Indian Law Resource Center
____ Louis W. Ballard
____ Navarro Scott Momaday
____ Will Rogers
____ Maria Tallchief

Exhibit 5. PIC Handout Order Form (front and back). This is mailed to faculty in various departments, including the departments of Sociology, Communications, and American Culture, and the Center for Africa & Afro-American Studies. Faculty members can order handouts appropriate to their specific classes.

Books By and About People of Color

Selected bibliographies on Literature by and about People of Color

____   Books By and About Asian Americans

____   Books By and About African American Authors of the Harlem Renaissance

____   Books By and About African American Women

____   Books By and About Latino Americans

____   Books By and About Native Americans

Other

____   Reference Works on the Arab World

____   Reference Works on Jewish Americans

____   Interracial Issues

 **PEER INFORMATION COUNSELING MATERIALS**

NAME:_____

CAMPUS ADDRESS:_____

_____

OFFICE TELEPHONE:_____

University Message System (MTS); please circle   UB   UM   NEITHER

UB or UM name if different from above:_____

Please mail to:
                    Karen Downing
                    122 Undergraduate Library 1185

# PIC...
Information
is our
middle name.

The Library is a bigger place than you think.
And Peer Information Counseling can help
you make the most of it.

We can give you a personal tour of the
Undergraduate Library, show you how to
find periodicals and other research materials,
even introduce you to a variety of word
processing programs.

Having trouble with that term paper? PIC
can show you some useful indexes and
reference books.

Want to learn about MIRLYN, the on-line
catalog? PIC can show you how to run your
own search.

So PIC up some good habits, and come see
us at the UGL Reference Desk.

Or PIC up the phone and leave a message on
the PIC-Line. 764-6849. Give us a call!

Peer Information Counseling is a service of
The University of Michigan Undergraduate Library.

Exhibit 6. Newspaper Advertisement for PIC. This paid advertisement ran in
the university newspaper.

Finding the Information You Need
another free service offered by Peer Information Counseling

I've lived in a small town all of my life, and I never saw a library that was larger than three rooms. Needless to say, I found the University of Michigan's library system overwhelming. I first used Peer Information Counseling when I needed to do a Psychology report, and I could not find any books. My RA recommended the service and I've used it ever since.

Cristina
Senior, Biology

PIC-Line
764-6849

What: Help finding books, articles, and other information.
Where: The Undergraduate Library
When: Every evening and most afternoons.
Stop by the Reference Desk or call 764-6849 for more information.

The University of Michigan Library, Undergraduate Library

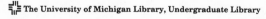

Exhibit 7. PIC Flyer/Poster. This flyer is one in a series of four flyers that were distributed to students and posted around campus to call attention to PIC.

Bibliography

Addressing Ethnic and Cultural Diversity: A Report on the Activities of the American Library Association, 1986–1989. Compiled and edited by Sibyl E. Moses. OLOS Report, no. 1, Chicago: American Library Association, 1990.

American Library Association, Association of College and Research Libraries, Bibliographic Instruction Section. "Cultural Diversity and Higher Education: BI in a Multicultural Environment." Preconference held at the annual meeting of the American Library Association, Atlanta, June 28, 1991.

American Library Association Presidential Committee on Information Literacy. *Final Report.* Chicago: American Library Association, January 1989.

Bluemel, Nancy Larson, and Rhonda Harris Taylor. "Saving Just One Student." *Book Report* 9 (January/February 1991), 36.

Bopp, Richard E., and Linda C. Smith. "Reference Services to Special Groups." In *Reference and Information Services: An Introduction.* Englewood, Colo.: Libraries Unlimited, 1991, 207–34.

Bradley, Jana. *Improving Written Communication in Libraries.* Chicago: American Library Association, 1988.

Breivik, Patricia. *Planning the Library Program.* Chicago: American Library Association, 1982.

Bringing Us Together: A Selected Guide to Cultural Diversity Activities in the Library Community. Chicago: American Library Association, President's Committee on Cultural Diversity, 1992.

Chatran, Richard. "Latino Reference Arrives." *American Libraries,* May 1987, 384–87.

Childress, Schelley H. "Training of Student Assistants in College Libraries: Some Insights and Ideas." *Arkansas Libraries* 44 (March 1987), 25–27.

Clark, Alice, and Kay F. Jones. "Writing Objectives: Methodology and Examples."
    In *Teaching Librarians to Teach*. Metuchen, N.J.: Scarecrow, 1986.
Commission on Minority Participation in Education and American Life. *One
    Third of a Nation*. Washington, D.C.: ACE/Education Commission of the
    States, 1988.
Cooper, Alan. *An Introduction to Statistics for Librarians*. Loughborough,
    Leicestershire: Centre for Library and Information Studies, Lough-
    borough University, 1982.
Cultural Diversity Programming in ARL Libraries. Spec Kit 165. Washington,
    D.C.: Association of Research Libraries, Office of Management Studies,
    1990.
Dawkins, Willie Mae, and Jeffrey Jackson. "Enhancing Reference Services:
    Students as Assistants." *Technicalities* 6, no. 8 (August 1986), 4–7.
Downing, Karen, and Jayashri Nagaraja. "Innovation and Outreach in Academic
    Libraries." Forthcoming.
Dyson, Alan. "Reaching Out for Outreach: A University Library Develops a New
    Position to Serve the School's Multicultural Students." *American
    Libraries*, November 1989, 952–54.
Egbers, Gail, and Joan Giesecke. "SPICE Programs in Nebraska: Minority High
    School Students in a University Setting." *C&RL News*, October 1989,
    840–43.
Evans, Charles. "A History of Community Analysis in American Librarianship."
    Library Trends 24, no. 3 (January 1976), 441–55.
Foley, May. "Reference and Information Services in a Multicultural Environ-
    ment." *Journal of Libraries and Information Science*, October 1984,
    143–62.
Freedman, Janet, and Harold Bantly. *Information Searching: A Handbook for
    Creating and Designing Instruction*. Metuchen, N.J.: Scarecrow, 1982.
Fuller, F. Jay. "Evaluating Student Assistants as Library Employees." *C&RL
    News* 51, no. 1 (January 1990), 11–13.
Goldhor, Herbert. "Community Analysis for the Public Library." *Illinois
    Libraries* 62, no. 4 (April 1980), 296–302.
Güereña, Salvador. "Community Analysis and Needs Assessment." In *Latino
    Librarianship: A Handbook for Professionals*. Jefferson, N.C.: Mc-
    Farland & Co., 1990, 17–23.
Hall, Patrick. "The Role of Affectivity in Instructing People of Color: Some
    Implications for Bibliographic Instruction." *Library Trends* 39, no. 3
    (Winter 1991), 316–26.
Hamilton, Feona. *Infopromotion: Publicity and Marketing Ideas for the Informa-
    tion Profession*. Brookfield, Vt.: Gower, 1990.
Hernon, Peter, and Charles R. McClure. *Evaluation and Library Decision
    Making*. Norwood, N.J.: Ablex Publishing, 1990.
Hernon, Peter, et al. *Statistics for Library Decision Making*. Norwood, N.J.: Ablex
    Publishing, 1989.

Hobbs, Daryl. "Strategy for Needs Assessment." In *Needs Assessment: Theory and Methods*. Edited by Donald E. Johnson et al. Ames: Iowa State University Press, 1987.

Huston, Mary M. "May I Introduce You: Teaching Culturally Diverse End-Users Through Everyday Information Seeking Experiences." *RSR* 17, no. 1 (Spring 1989), 8–11.

Jackson, Bailey, and Evangelina Holvino. *Multicultural Organization Development*. PCMA Working Paper #11; CRSO Working Paper #356. Ann Arbor: University of Michigan, Center for Research on Social Organization, 1988.

Janes, Phoebe, and Ellen Meltzer. "Origins and Attitudes: Training Reference Librarians for a Pluralistic World." In *Continuing Education of Reference Librarians*. New York: Haworth Press, 1990, 145–55.

Jones, Kay F. "Multicultural Diversity and the Academic Library." *Urban Academic Librarian* 8, no. 1 (Winter 1990/1991), 14–22.

Keiser, Barbie E., and Carol K. Galvin. *Marketing Library Services: A Nuts-and-Bolts Approach*. Sudbury, Mass.: Riverside Data, 1988.

Kflu, Tesfai, and Mary A. Loomba. "Academic Libraries and the Culturally Diverse Student Population." *C&RL News*, June 1990, 524–27.

Kirk, Thomas. "Problems in Library Instruction in Four-Year Colleges." In *Educating the Library User*. Edited by John Lubans, Jr. New York: Bowker, 1974.

Kravitz, Lesley, Adela Terres Rios, and Vivian B. Sykes. "Documenting Their Voices: Building Library Collections for the New Majority." *Journal of Library Administration and Management*, November 1991.

Kuh, George D., and Elizabeth J. Whit. *The Invisible Tapestry: Culture in American Colleges and Universities*. ASHE-ERIC Higher Education Reports, 1988.

Lam, Errol. "The Reference Interview: Some Intercultural Considerations." *RQ*, Spring 1988, 390–93.

Lawton, Bethany. "Library Instruction Needs Assessment: Designing Survey Instruments." *Research Strategies* 7, no. 3 (Summer 1989), 119–128.

Lewis, Jerry J. "The Black Freshman Network." *College & University* 61, no. 2 (Winter 1986), 135–40.

Lubans, John, Jr. "Evaluating Library-User Education Programs." In *Educating the Library User*. Edited by John Lubans, Jr. New York: Bowker, 1977.

MacAdam, Barbara, and Darlene Nichols. "Peer Information Counseling: An Academic Library Program for Minority Students." *Journal of Academic Librarianship* 15 (September 1989), 204–9.

———. "Peer Information Counseling at the University of Michigan Undergraduate Library." *Journal of Academic Librarianship*, May 1988, 80–81.

Mensching, Theresa B., ed. *Reaching and Teaching Diverse Library User Groups*. Ann Arbor, Mich.: Pierian Press, 1989.

Newhouse, Robert. "A Library Essential: Needs Assessment." *Library Reviews* 39, no. 2 (1990), 33–36.

Noel, L. "College Retention—A Campus-Wide Responsibility." *Journal of the National Association of College Admissions Counselors* 21 (1976), 33–36.

Ortiz, Isidro, and Salvador Güreña. "The Co-production of Library Services for Racial Minorities: A Feasible Task." *Alternative Librarian Literature,* 1984–1985, 99–106.

Ostrow, Rona, and Sweetman R. Smith. *The Dictionary of Marketing.* New York: Fairchild Publications, 1988.

Point of Intersection: The University Library and the Pluralistic Campus Community: A Report to the Vice Provost for Minority Affairs on University Library Programs for Enhancing Diversity and Academic Excellence at the University of Michigan. Ann Arbor: University of Michigan Library, November 18, 1988.

Porter, Oscar F. *Undergraduate Completion and Persistence at Four-Year Colleges and Universities: Detailed Findings.* Washington, D.C.: National Institute of Independent Colleges and Universities, 1990.

Powell, Ronald. *Basic Research Methods for Librarians.* Norwood, N.J.: Ablex Publishing, 1991.

Renford, Beverly, and Linnea Hendrickson. *Bibliographic Instruction: A Handbook.* New York: Neal-Schuman, 1980.

Report of the President's Committee on Library Services to Minorities. Equity at Issue: Library Services to the Nation's Four Major Minority Groups. Chicago: American Library Association, 1986.

Rice, James, Jr. *Teaching Library Use.* Westport, Conn.: Greenwood Press, 1981.

Richardson, Richard C., and Elizabeth Fisk Skinner. *Achieving Quality and Diversity: Universities in a Multicultural Society.* New York: American Council on Education, 1991.

Ridgeway, Trish. "Information Literacy: An Introductory Reading List." *C&RL News,* July/August 1990, 645–48.

Roberts, Anne F., and Susan G. Blandy. *Library Instruction for Librarians.* Englewood, Colo.: Libraries Unlimited, 1989.

Rothman, Jack, and Larry Gant. "Approaches and Models of Community Intervention." In *Needs Assessment: Theory and Methods.* Edited by Donald E. Johnson et al. Ames: Iowa State University Press, 1987.

Russel, John H., and Rodney R. Skinkle. "Evaluation of Peer Advisor Effectiveness." *Journal of College Student Development,* September 1990, 388–93.

Shavit, David. "Qualitative Evaluation of Reference Service." *Reference Librarian,* no. 11 (Fall/Winter 1984).

Shields, Gerald R., and J. Gordon Burke, comp. *Budgeting for Accountability in Libraries: A Selection of Readings.* Metuchen, N.J.: Scarecrow, 1974.

Simmons, R., and C. Maxwell-Simmons. *Principles of Success in Programs for Minority Students*. Hoboken, N.J.: Stevens Institute of Technology, 1978.

Simpson, I. S. *Basic Statistics for Librarians*. London: Clive Bingley, 1983.

Slater, Margaret, ed. *Research Methods in Library and Information Studies*. London: Library Association, 1990.

Solmon, Lewis, and Tamara Wingard. "The Changing Demographics: Problems and Opportunities." In *The Racial Crisis in American Higher Education*. Edited by Philip G. Altbach and Kofi Lomotey. Albany: State University of New York Press, 1991.

Spotts, Bethany L. "Creating a Successful Minority Affairs Position." *Journal of College Admission*, Spring 1991, 4–9.

Stoffle, Carla J. "A New Library for the New Undergraduate." *Library Journal* 115, no. 16 (October 1, 1990), 47–51.

Tinto, Vincent. *Leaving College: Rethinking the Causes and Cures of Student Attrition*. Chicago: University of Chicago Press, 1987.

Treyillo, Robert G., and David C. Weber. "Academic Library Responses to Cultural Diversity: A Position Psper for the 1990's." *Journal of Academic Librarianship* 17, no. 3 (July 1991), 157–62.

Trumpeter, Margo C., and Richard S. Rourds. *Basic Budgeting Practices for Librarians*. Chicago: American Library Association, 1985.

U.S. National Commission on Excellence in Education. *A Nation at Risk*. Washington, D.C.: Government Printing Office, 1983.

University of Texas at Austin. General Libraries. *Comprehensive Program of User Education for the General Libraries*. Austin: University of Texas at Austin, General Libraries, 1977.

Walter, Allen. "Black Colleges vs. White Colleges: The Fork in the Road for Black Students." *Change* 19 (May/June 1987), 28–34.

Weingand, Darlene E. *Marketing/Planning Library and Information Services*. Littleton, Colo.: Libraries Unlimited, 1987.

Westbrook, Lynn. *Qualitative Evaluation Methods for Reference Services: An Introductory Manual*. Washington, D.C.: Association of Research Libraries, 1989.

————. "Students and Support Staff on the Reference Desk." *C&RL News* 50, no. 9 (October 1989), 808–10.

Widdows, Richard, Tia Hensler, and Marlaya Wyncott. "The Focus Group: A Method for Assessing Users' Evaluation of Library Service." *College and Research Libraries* 54, no. 4 (July 1991), 354.

Wilder, Stanley. "Library Jobs and Student Retention." *C&RL News* 51, no. 11 (December 1990), 1035–38.

Wood, Elizabeth J., and Victoria L. Young. *Strategic Marketing for Libraries: A Handbook*. Westport, Conn.: Greenwood Press, 1988.

Index

About the Authors

KAREN E. DOWNING is Associate Librarian and Coordinator of Academic Outreach Services at the University of Michigan Undergraduate Library.

BARBARA MacADAM is Head of the Undergraduate Library at the University of Michigan. She has published in journals such as *College and Research Libraries, The Reference Librarian,* and the *Journal of Academic Librarianship.*

DARLENE P. NICHOLS is Associate Librarian at the University of Michigan Undergraduate Library. Her publications include articles on Peer Information Counseling in the *Journal of Academic Librarianship.*